See you at the crossroads!
Uri Campbell

Vic Campbell

Junction:

County Road 197

Mild Adventure for the Armchair Ruralist

Contributed Essays: D. H. Cummings and C. G. Wade, Jr.

Illustrations: Nancy Akin

Xander Creek Press
Sparta, New Jersey
1992

Xander Creek Press
1992

Three Fairway Trail, Sparta, New Jersey 07871

LIBRARY OF CONGRESS CATALOGING-IN-PUBLICATION DATA

Campbell, Vic. 1949-

Junction: county road 197 (mild adventure for the armchair ruralist)
by Vic Campbell.

Series of articles reprinted from the Santa Rosa County Press Gazette,
1985-1989

ISBN 0-933776-32-2
    1. Santa Rosa County (Fla.)—Social life and customs.
    2. Campbell, Vic., 1949-   .
    3. Santa Rosa County (Fla.)—Biography.
    I. Title.
    F317.S4C35 1992
    975.19'985—dc20   89-16209
                                           CIP

To My Mother and Father

Myrtle and J. Lee

Contents

LOVE ★ WAR ★ ROMANCE ★ ADVENTURE LAUGHTER ★ TEARS

A CAST OF HUNDREDS OF REAL PEOPLE

"I laughed loud and often.
Beware though, sometimes the humor
bites--leaving a lump in your throat.
A sad story can hide behind the very next
page and catch you off-guard."

"This 'Southern' experience is really
a universal one."

Report Cards

"Victor is a fine student. Reads very well. Understands his numbers work—
works independently—finishes work—has a very good personality. His
attendance from Sept. to Nov. 21 has been 66 days."

11-30-56 Camilla Lux
2nd Grade, Pacific View School
San Diego County, California

"Am helping Victor to do better printing."

2-20-57 Bobbie Whitley
2nd Grade, Chumuckla School
Santa Rosa County, Florida
Neil R. Childers, Principal

"Victor has been nice to work with."

6-3-59 Dovie Stewart
4th Grade, Chumuckla School
Santa Rosa County, Florida
William H. Massey, Principal

"Victor is lazy, working only hard enough to get by, or to obtain certain
privileges. As a result he is wasting wonderful God-given talent."

6-6-60 Alfred T. Williams
5th Grade, Chumuckla School
Santa Rosa County, Florida
John E. Temple, Principal

ACKNOWLEDGMENTS

This book is a collection of columns that appeared in The Press Gazette, the premier news media for all of Santa Rosa County, Florida. Most were written and published between 1985 and 1989. I am thankful to the people at The Press Gazette—Wanda Lockett for encouraging my writing for the newspaper column and Rich Barrett for allowing it to run right up front on the "Op Ed" page.

Grateful thanks to my editor, Jean Rabe, whose work, under the name "Red Pen," is normally editing of a more technical nature. Jean also took on the task of setting the type and graphics for this book, a contribution that deserves not only thanks, but a large measure of praise.

Thanks to family and friends who encouraged and assisted with ideas and especially to my wife, Karen, for allowing me to test her good nature. A special appreciation to my sister Wanda Roberts and my brother Jim for lifelong friendships. If someone else had been my brother and sister, I would have grown up with complete strangers. An added measure of love to my mother and father, who helped me to make memories; to grandparents who helped me appreciate them; to aunts and uncles who brightened them; and to cousins who shared them with my brother and sister and me.

Many of the people who helped build the memories that colored this book—and whose names are enscribed here—are now gone. I am grateful for having known them.

Special thanks to the following people who contributed historical accuracies and vintage photographs: Beverly and Cynthia Campbell, Joyce Hatfield, the family of Roy and

Velvie Hatfield, Voncille Burgess, C. G. Wade, Bernadine Howard, Elizabeth Matthews, Robert Jones, John S. Brown, and posthumously to "Rusty" Grundin. Additional photographs came from family archives.

Computer transfers were accomplished by Joy Britt and Sharon Karnick. Their work is appreciated. Production and graphics were largely inspired by L. Bart Ruggiero. His advice was invaluable.

The illustrations by Nancy Akin and the contributions of Dianne Hatfield Cummings and Coleman (Junior) Wade add a depth I could not have achieved alone. Dianne and "Junior" wrote the next-to-last section of the book.

Thanks also to Tom Carter for the cover photo and my portrait. My sense of style was greatly enhanced by my Aunt Frances, who loaned me Uncle Duke's wool shirt for the photograph that Tom took of me. About the cover photo: Carnley's Store at Chumuckla Crossroads, Autumn 1991, is owned by Andy and Leigh Ann Carnley. The truck is a 1987 Chevrolet Silverado with a stock 350 V-8 engine. It is owned and piloted by "Rusty" Pierce (Bull's Woodshop in Jay). It is for sale.

And finally, I thank Dr. Bill Coker for guidance on publishing and my Uncle, E. W. Carswell, who set an example of authorship—and kept me from being killed at a World War II Army veteran's reunion in North Carolina, where I wore my Navy ball cap and suggested that the Navy was a snappier branch of service!

INTRODUCTION

E. W. Carswell

Vic Campbell has illuminated the map of Chumuckla. Just about everyone who has read his newspaper columns, wherever they may be—East Texas, Northern New Jersey, West Florida, or West Germany—knows that Chumuckla is (or was) the home of Pug Carnley's Grocery and Gas Station.

Newspapers no longer need mention that Chumuckla is in Florida. They must assume that Chumuckla—like Chicago, Harlem, Chappaquiddick, Chicamauga, Berrydale Crossroads, and Atlanta—is too well known to need further identification. So, they don't explain that the Creek Indian word "Chumuklita," which is said to mean "to bow the head to the ground," implies the existence of an early place to worship.

To the Indians, then, Chumuckla must have been some sort of a holy place (local tradition favors a translation of "Healing Waters"). It still may be for the Campbells and their kin. Hundreds live near Chumuckla, including Coon Hill, Brownsdale, Ward's Store, Allentown, Three Hollows Branch, Floridatown, and Mulat communities. They are all Vic's cousins to some degree. And, he has written about all of them. He has hundreds of cousins—in other parts of West Florida and in Alabama; and he has written about some of them.

You'll meet some of his cousins and other neighbors in this book, in which many of them are mentioned. They seem to be as well-known to some of Vic's readers in New Jersey as they are to his former neighbors in West Florida and places in between and beyond.

They're also familiar with Pond Creek, Parker Island, the Jay Livestock Market, and Two-Toed Tom—that awesome alligator in Esto's Sand Hammock Lake. Vic heard the legend of Two-Toed Tom from his Uncle "Tobe," whose home—along with those of a lot of Vic's other maternal kinsmen—was once beside Sand Hammock Lake.

Vic has an unusual—some say weird—sense of humor. But he is not afraid to laugh at himself. Some of his readers say his brand of humor is an antidote to so much drab, dreary, dismally depressing and scary news. For some, on the other hand, his humor takes awhile getting used to. He and his Uncle "Tobe" found that out at a veteran's convention once at Fort Bragg, North Carolina. But that episode is not in this book.

PREFACE

This is not a history. That sort of work can be left to my uncle, E. W. Carswell, who has chronicled the history of the Florida Panhandle.

He and people like Dr. Bill Coker at the University of West Florida, Dr. Brian Rucker, Earle Bowden of the _Pensacola News Journal_, and the late M. L. King are historians. Warren Weeks is an important local historian. They care a great deal about the _exactness_ of time and place. I commend them for it.

Some readers felt I might be a qualified historian because I mention real people and real events. Too often, although the events are real enough, they are warped beyond recognition when electronically recorded from the cerebral cortex of an individual with unlicensed imagination.

The names often belong to very real people—even though it is not unusual that they, themselves, do not recognize the incidents in which I have placed them. That explains why I cannot be taken seriously as a historical reference.

It is the "flavor" of the times as I saw them—sometimes funny, very funny—sometimes not at all funny. Somewhere, between the laughter and the tears, there is a real world. We live it every day. In time, the real events in a real world fade into an unsure memory. It is only the flavor of an unsure memory that you will capture from this book.

Some years ago, I began to write as an outlet for the frustrations of a corporate cowboy. A friend encouraged my hometown newspaper, _The Press Gazette_, to carry a weekly column. Over time, the writing became a weekly vacation for my mind—a chance to be a little closer to home, to rekindle old friendships and to express my own inner thoughts.

Sooner than I could think about it, there were enough columns for a book—the first collection.

I

As It Was in the Beginning
Is Now
and Ever Shall Be

—I reckon.

"The more things change, the more they remain the same."

"The Thing that hath been, is that which shall be;
and that which is done is that which shall be done;
and there is no new thing under the sun."

Ecclesiastes 1:9

JUSTICE IN MY TIME...

Fourth Grade is a trying time for most nine-year olds.

Mrs. Dovie Stewart will tell you that it is even more trying for the teacher. She taught Fourth Grade until she retired in 1979.

Our Fourth Grade class at Chumuckla School was a scholarly group. We studied the mul-

tiplication tables and committed them to memory. I still remember some. For instance, 4 x 4 is a vehicle that can travel over almost any terrain, while 2 x 4 is a stick of lumber that is really only 1.5 x 3.5 inches.

We absorbed lessons in Social Studies. In these classes, we learned for the first time that there were other *counties* besides our own. There were other countries too. The people looked different from us. They wore different clothes; they spoke different languages. In general, they were very strange.

"The Incident" happened during one of Mrs. Stewart's comparative sociology lectures. She was explaining the similarities between uncivilized tribes of Papua, New Guinea, and the jungle social order of Manhattan Island. Her nephew, Paul, turned to me at the desk behind him and wiped an unhealthy dose of nasal discharge on my shirt sleeve.

The act was a shock to my sensibilities and to my sensitive nature! If I had known the words, I would have said to myself, "This is abhorrent social behavior and it is thoroughly disgusting." But, I did not.

1

Paul's Aunt Dovie did not see him do the foul act. If she had, I'm sure she would have whacked the daylights out of him. Although she failed to see Paul's reprehensible behavior, she did see my response to it.

I "picked" a suitable retaliatory weapon and inflicted the loathsome thing on Paul's arm. "Victor, you come outside class with me this minute!" exclaimed Mrs. Stewart.

I was in trouble, and I knew it. I had escalated a "smelly" situation into an "armed" conflict. Mrs. Stewart was about to hold a "Summit Conference" with me, and the outcome did not appear propitious in my regard. In fact, it was not.

Mrs. Stewart never knew that Paul started the incident. I have kept the dark secret until this very day.

The Chumuckla High Class of 1967 (17 graduating members) will hold its twenty-year reunion in June of this year (1987). I hope to see Paul there. I hope his Aunt Dovie shows up, too.

"Ne Obliviscaris" (Never Forget) is the motto of "The Campbell Clan." Well, I have not forgotten. At our class reunion, I will explain the incident in light of historical perspective. I hope Paul's Aunt Dovie will whack his backside until the sun goes down.

"Did so do it, Paul!" says I. "Did not!" says Paul.

"Did done it." "Didn't done it."

"Did." "Didn't."

§§§§§§§

2

WE WHISTLE WHILE WE WORK

In the second grade at Chumuckla School when Mrs. Whitley caught me whistling in class. It was my first whistle. Before that time, I could not emit one whit.

I was years behind my colleagues. Nearly all had learned to whistle by the age of five. Some had learned as early as age two.

Benny Enfinger had a cousin who once stayed overnight with a friend who had an aunt whose father-in-law once marched in a parade in New York City. While there, he had learned the "fingers-in-mouth" method of whistling for a taxi cab. The lesson filtered down through acquaintances and generations until Benny learned "The Method" as well.

Compared with Benny's, my life was a glaring failure. I could not whistle. Even "Junior" Wade could whistle well enough to imitate a sick meadowlark. Jimmy Utley could imitate Junior's imitation of a sick meadowlark. And Joan Bell (a Girl!) could whistle as well as anyone.

I could not gain the respect of my peers until I had mastered the art of whistling. Given any opportunity, I would practice.

I practiced during hymns at church. It must have been disconcerting to the adults who observed me out of the corners of their eyes. I was not singing, but puffing my cheeks and blowing soundless air out of my puckered lips.

I practiced in the church graveyard. I hoped the ghostly inspiration would bring forth sound as I desperately pushed moist air between my teeth and lips.

I tried to learn from my big brother, whose two front teeth were as big as split-cedar shingles. The gap between his teeth allowed him to whistle with an amazing tonal quality. My own teeth were not gapped the same way, and no amount of coaching from my brother would help.

Then it happened. In a quiet study period, in the second grade classroom, as I woefully traced the letter "R" over and over and over again on my three-line writer's tablet with a giant lead pencil, my dream was at last achieved. As if by magic, a piercing whistle exuded from my puckered lips.

Every kid in the classroom looked up from their boring assignment of drawing "Rs" and looked to the source of the sound. Mrs. Whitley admonished, "Now, Victor. We do not whistle in class. Be quiet or I'll have to punish you."

The year was 1957. In those times, teachers were the next closest thing to the President of the United States of America. They even had a picture of George Washington on the wall behind their desks as if to reinforce their place in the chain of command. Teachers were respected in those days.

Obviously, however, she did not appreciate the significance of the momentous thing that had just occurred. I could not withhold another effort now. Not for all the respect in the whole world! The "Force" was with me.

"Wh...Whoo...Wheee...Whis...Whis-tle...whistle, whistle, whistle."

There! I had done it. I now had the correct lip contortion locked into memory. From that day forward, I would be able to impress my friends with the sounds of the birds of the air and the wolves of the streets.

4

I was an equal of my classmates. I was whole. The world was a brighter place to be. I would meet life with a song in my heart and a whistle on my lips.

And—a paddle on my behind. I took my punishment, but it was worth it.

§§§§§§

THE GREAT FISH HUNT...1964

We had everything we needed for a good camping trip. Our cardboard box was full—tin-foil, paper towels, matches, cast iron skillet, and Irish potatoes. We had all the assorted paraphernalia of the camping trade—and we planned to catch fish.

But, for insurance you understand, we relieved the home freezer of four sirloin steaks. I think they were part of "Ol' Buster," a steer we butchered the previous February. All was tossed without ceremony into the bed of our blue Ford F-100 stepside pickup truck. A musty bale of hay remained there from our latest trip to "The Back Forty". It held the cardboard box in place. Brother Jim drove because he was sixteen.

Leaving behind the world of concerns our parents and teachers had tried unsuccessfully to impose on our young lives, we struck out for Keyser's Landing on the Delaney River. Floyd and Neal Enfinger joined us on this excursion. They met us at the river.

5

Jim and Neal slipped a boat in the water just before dark. They moved slowly and quietly "up river" to set out trot-lines. They attached treble hooks and baited them with the insides of dead chickens. We hoped their invested effort would bring a harvest of succulent catfish before the light of dawn.

Floyd and I set up camp and prepared our cane poles for serious bank fishing. We had an old Maxwell House coffee can full of worms. I had collected the fresh red wigglers that same afternoon from underneath Grandma's massive camphor tree. The well- fertilized tree grew behind her house, next to the chicken yard.

The worms did not make the effort to do their job as well as they should. Of course, it could have been the noise Floyd made as he whispered brief monologues, commenting on the weather, school, and girls. We were not of an age, yet, to discuss politics. I convinced myself that Floyd was scaring the fish away.

I hollered, "SHUDD-UP FLOYD-OYd-oyd ... YOU'RE GONNA SCARE THE FISH-ISH-ISh-ish!" The echo re-turned across the peaceful river water, bouncing off a solid wall of moss-covered Cypress trees on the eerie shores of snake- infested Parker Island. Soon, Floyd would forget and whisper again. I had to yell at him several times.

Luck was not forthcoming with conventional fresh water angling. I pondered our situation. Using astute empirical analysis, I arrived at a solution. WE WOULD SHOOT THE FISH.

Floyd and I went back to the truck. We pulled out a flash-light and an old Sears & Roebuck single-shot 22-caliber rifle. By this time, it was inky dark. Floyd and I followed the river trail until we found a likely place to shoot our fish. Floyd held the light and spotted for me. The fish appeared to sit motionless in awe of the beam, quietly awaiting their execution.

I aimed and fired: CRACK-ACk-Ack-ack! A plume of water rose into the air—but no fish. Shooting fish appeared to be an easy job, but it wasn't working for us. Science now tells me that the fish were not where we thought we saw them because of light refraction and because the water deflected our bullets. The chances of our shooting a fish were about zero.

But nature had thrown down the gauntlet. Our purpose in life (for that moment) was to meet the challenge.

We made another trip back to the truck. From underneath the seat, I reverently resurrected "Pop's Pride and Joy". It was a double-barrelled, engraved "Baretta", 12-gauge, shot gun. He bought it in Naples, Italy, on his last cruise aboard the U.S.S Shangri-La. I slipped it out of its protective case. It was a thing of beauty. My calculations suggested a load of single ought buckshot would have better odds of striking a fish than would a solitary round fired from a 22-caliber rifle.

Again, Floyd and I looked for a prime location from which to blast our prey. We slipped down a clay bank and stood at the water's edge by a rotting log of Paleozoic proportions.

Floyd shined the light on a monstrous catfish. I figured a fish this size must have survived in these waters since the Devonian period of prehistory. It was Delaney River's equivalent of the Lochness monster. It was lying about 16 inches beneath the surface of the water, near the log. I loaded one barrel with buckshot. I prepared to take aim. To support myself, and to steady my sights, I looked down to place my foot on the "prehistoric" log below.

"SNAKE-AKE-Ake-ake!", I bellowed. The echo resonated in the humid swamp air. BLAM-AM-Am-am! The gun fired into the air. Buckshot scattered the width and breadth of the serpentine haven of Parker Island.

From the top of the small cliff, Floyd and I could see the Cotton Mouth Moccasin. The venomous reptile slipped easily into the river water beside the fresh footprints beneath us. The air grew still. When Jim and Neal returned, the steaks were done to perfection.

∮∮∮∮∮∮

SAUTÉ WITH WHISKEY UNTIL DONE...

When my brother, Jim, was fourteen years old, and I was thirteen, he found a bottle of whiskey in our pasture beside "Scared Man's Curve." We have called it "Scared Man's Curve" ever since Jim found the bottle of "Johnny Walker." We figured some scared man threw it out of his car as an arm (and perhaps a leg, too) of the law pursued him through the county.

We knew we were too young to drink the elixir. On the other hand, we knew we were too old to tell our parents about it. So, we saved it for a couple of years. Somewhere, we had heard aged whiskey is superior in quality.

The time we judged to be correct was the summer my brother turned sixteen. We took the bottle with us on a camping trip to our favorite place, "Keyser's Landing." We sat around the campfire with our friend, Teddy "Two-Toe" Turnipseed (a near world class master at the hazardous game of barefoot mumblety peg). Teddy was also a mature sixteen. We discussed how we should dispose of the whiskey.

We were all in agreement that the substance should be consumed. That point was settled early on. Negotiations began in earnest over who would get the first drink and who would get the most.

We argued over a secrecy agreement and decided that we were prohibited from telling anyone about the whiskey for our whole lives. We were not to tell our wives—should we ever marry, or our Sunday School teachers—should they ask if ever we had sinned.

"No, Miss Lavita, ma'am. I ain't never smoked no cigarettes or drank no alcohol ... much ... to speak of."

A major problem developed in trying to divide the whiskey equally among the three of us. The bottle was a fifth of a gallon, whatever that was. And, there were three of us. It is not easy to divide one fifth by three.

Nobody thought to bring cups, so we had to improvise a drinking vessel. I dumped our fishing worms out of the rusty coffee can. I rinsed it out in the river. "Two Toe" took some of the ice from the cooler that held our steaks and our frozen catalpa worms. Jim cracked the seal on the bottle and let us all sniff the aroma of alcohol.

A small amount of whiskey was poured into the can. Jim was the first to taste it because he had found the bottle. As was the custom portrayed in the movies, he took a quick gulp. His face turned red. He gagged and he choked. Red liquid oozed from the corners of his mouth. We thought he

9

was going to die. Only later did we discover that the liquid was colored by rust from the worm can chalice.

When he stood up and yelled, "Water! Water! Get me water!" his foot tipped the bottle. Nearly all the remaining whiskey poured out on the ground. Only a minuscule portion of the precious forbidden substance remained.

"Two Toe" made mention of the fact that refined people cook with wine. It made sense that we might cook our steaks in whiskey, providing thereby a similar result. The pleasant effect would be that we could all partake of the liquid, what little remained. And "Two Toe" and I would probably fare better than had my afflicted brother, Jim.

So we poured the few drops that remained on top of our frozen steaks. We cooked them over red hot coals until the steaks were charcoal black. They were among the first-ever "Cajun Steaks"—only they were burned through and through. Steaks are best, I believe, when burned to cinders and then smothered in ketchup.

We each felt the arrangement was fair. I have never tasted a steak that was as good as the one we ate that night: sautéed in whiskey. Each of us swore to the others that he was drunk. We even complained among ourselves of exorbitant hangovers the next morning.

$$\oint\oint\oint\oint\oint\oint\oint$$

A SONGBIRD MEMORY

It was 1961. I was eleven years old. Whether I wanted to or not, I had to go to church on Sunday. A person who did not go to church was considered a borderline Communist—or at the very least, un-American. If you were eleven years old and not in church, your prospects of a happy future were grim. In our home your immediate future held prospects of a persimmon switch fanned hot with the fire of brimstone.

In that year, the church had not yet gained enough stature, or money, to buy the white oak pews that today grace the sanctuary. The pews were made of wooden pine slats, stained brown. They were comfortable in the summer. Air could circulate all through the backs and under the seat to battle any amount of heat produced by the climate or the preacher.

In the winter, two gas heaters, one on either side of the altar, near the front pew, kept the faithful warm. In winter Preacher Renfroe found a warm and friendly congregation of about forty people crowding the front rows. Everybody wanted a front-row seat.

Regardless of my desperate attempts to avoid the ritual of wearing a tie and shining my shoes for the sake of proper looks, or the thoughts of impending boredom with the preacher's sermons, I actually quite enjoyed the Sunday interludes.

One of my favorite things was to read the comments written in the back of the Cokesbury hymnals that were stacked at every pew. While I read the penciled commentaries (Ann loves Troy, Bill is a two-timer, a heart drawn with the intials written in about who loved who, and a joke about the chicken and the pig), our choir would give a never-to-be-repeated, one-of-a-kind performance. I did not pay much attention.

I do, however, recall my cousins Ann, Mary, and Brenda Howell singing as a quartet with their mother, Juanita. The music would drift gently over pews and under the window sills to the back pew where I was deep in thought, studying the encrypted messages scribbled on the illustrated cardboard fans supplied by the funeral parlor.

They sang songs that normal people could relate to: "Bringing in the Sheaves," which I envisioned as something like hauling in the hay; "The Old Rugged Cross," which some of us irreverently altered to a song about an old Chevrolet; and "We Shall Gather By The River," which painted for me a picture of the Escambia River in full flood. It was going to be mighty hard for some of us to get to the other side.

The music was simple. The people were genuine. Sometimes I think there is not enough of either any more. And sometimes the old harmony of the Howell sisters will haunt me, as I dream of a simpler time in the warm Sundays of my youth.

ƒƒƒƒƒƒƒ

RANCID MAYONNAISE AND SNAKE

Joe Cook. You know—Wheeler's boy, Voncille's brother. It was Joe who joined me on an equestrian outing one spring day in a long-ago memory. Joe was one of the brave few who would ride the crazy horses we kept on the farm. Sometimes the Cotton boy, Ronnie, would ride. And, if Danny Holt had not been nearly killed by one, he would have joined me more often.

It was a pleasant ride to Webb Landing, on the Escambia River. Peaceful and quiet, except for the muffled sounds of unshod ungulates. In those days, I must have had better ears. I can remember hearing birds voice the timeless notes of springtime. I can remember the sound of a "rain crow" announcing a drop in barometric pressure. The sounds of nature marched as an order of insects into battle with the stilled air.

My olfactory senses were better then too. The smell of honeysuckle in bloom would shout it's ownership of the surrounding atmosphere. Bay leaves there. Cypress here. And newly plowed ground. Fresh earth turned hours before, to this day leaves my senses refreshed.

As Joe and I rode, we unconsciously tuned in to a natural world that would record itself in the deepest parts of our young memories. Time invested this way provides a lifetime library of sensory perception.

Joe spotted the snake first. He had the vision of an eagle. He did not have to wear glasses. I did. Besides, my glasses were perpetually dirty. They still are.

It was a very unusual snake. Neither of us had ever seen one like it. Only its tail was exposed, hanging out over the drainage ditch beside the sandy, dirt road. It was black, with longitudinal red stripes extending the length of its body. The reptile was rotund, and yet it was long. It stretched almost five feet.

I found an appropriately long stick as quickly as I could dismount and thrash the bushes on the road opposite the reptilian prize. Then, I cornered the animal for capture. A little pressure on its neck and I picked it up. The eyes were round; it was not a viper. Obviously, it was not a coral snake because of its coloration. As amateur herpetologists, we knew immediately it was not a venomous snake.

I patiently introduced the nervous, wide-eyed horses to the cool, round-eyed snake. And soon we were on our way again. I held the snake in one hand, the other hand free to control the horse.

Near the river we found a wide-mouth, gallon mayonnaise jar—a discard from an inconsiderate camper. We rinsed it out and used it to store our pet. With a gallon of fresh snake, and the odor of stale mayonnaise, our two-horse expedition returned to base camp. Home. Civilization.

With the help of a reference book, we determined that it was a member of the genus Abastor, species erythrogrammus. The book suggested we were lucky to find it. The "rainbow snake" is quite shy, according to the authorities. Few people ever see one in the wild.

Joe carried our valuable find home with him. He was going to build a wire cage for it. As a temporary measure, he sequestered the shy reptile in a cardboard box under his bed. But the snake disappeared overnight. It was never seen again, not in the mobile home the Cooks lived in, or anywhere near it. After all, it was a shy snake. The Cooks were a nervous family for awhile. I think Wheeler steered Joe to other, less controversial, interests.

That was the last time I rode a horse down to the Escambia River. But, the sights, the smells, the sounds—and the snake—made a lasting impression.

§§§§§§§

14

MASSACRE AT COON HILL CEMETERY...

Yes, I was present at "The Coon Hill Massacre of 1965." It was very nearly an awful sight. It almost made the papers. And if it had actually occurred the way it appeared during moments of terrified imagination that Halloween night, it would have been headline material for sure.

If I hadn't invited Junior Wade, the whole thing would probably have blown over in a minute. Junior was onto the operation from the start. As soon as he crawled in the back of the pickup truck, I began to explain the mystery of Offal Skidmore, the disgraced brain surgeon turned hermit and mass murderer, who hid out in the swamps around Coon Hill.

The others were falling for the story. Earl Cox paid special attention to the saga. The pupils of his eyes grew larger and larger as my brother, Jim, repeated the part where Offal forced his victims to scrub behind their ears before he "opened their minds," so to speak.

When we stopped to pick up Ezel Lowery, Junior slipped out of the truck for a minute. He talked Ezel into loaning him an eight-inch "Bowie knife" and then hid the knife in his left sock, under his pants leg. He strapped it to his leg with a strip of rubber from an old bicycle inner tube.

Unknown to our passengers, but known to us, a fright crew had already been posted at the cemetery. Our scare squad included Carl Griffin, John Kimbrough, Ronnie Cotton,

Benny Enfinger, and Jimmy Saulz. They were stationed in strategic locations throughout the graveyard.

Darkness coated the scene when we arrived with our quarry. As we walked about the cemetery, skirting the tombstones, the chilled air wrapped its tendrils around our very souls. We had just finished wondering aloud about the whereabouts of poor old hermit Offal, when John Kimbrough jumped up with a flashlight shining under his chin and yelled "You gonna die."

He began to come for Earl, and Earl started to back off. Junior was concerned, but kept his mind clear with the thought of the knife on his leg. Then Benny Enfinger appeared from behind a tombstone and let out a hysterical laugh that left a reverberating echo in the swamps around us.

As John and Benny came for the group, Carl Griffin joined in. Earl knew it was a hoax at that point, because he recognized Carl's voice. Only, it was then that a shadowy figure emerged from another corner of the graveyard, descended on Carl, flashed a long blade in the moonlight, and appeared—from the angle of view—to impale Carl on the gleaming shaft. Earl logically figured this was not a part of the game. After all, who would be out to scare the scarERS.

All the scarEES had been in the truck with us. Earl assumed he had just seen his friend Carl die. Within milliseconds, he was over the cemetery wall and deep in the swamp, taking his chances with snakes and panthers. He figured Offal Skidmore was now among us, performing his butchery.

Junior had his knife out when Ronnie Cotton jumped from the shadows. When Ronnie said "Boo," Junior said, "Be still and shuddup or I'm a gonna cut off parts of your body." Ronnie swallowed hard and said, "Just jokin', Junior."

16

Junior and Ronnie made a quick pact to make Ronnie appear dead from the big knife. Then Junior held up the knife, with ketchup all over his hands and all over Ronnie and said, "I killed him."

Nobody expected one of the scarEES to have a knife. When the "chief scarERS," John and Carl and Jimmie (Offal) Saulz, saw the "dead" Ronnie, they lost their composure and began to beg Junior not to kill anybody else. Junior ran around loose in the graveyard for some time, yelling, "Come near me and I'll kill you." He was quite convincing, and Ronnie wasn't moving. Ezel was beginning to feel sorry he had loaned the knife to Junior.

The end came when Ronnie realized he was lying in a bed of black ants. The ants tired rather hurriedly of the ketchup and began feasting on Ronnie's adolescent skin. The more Ronnie yelled, the deeper Earl pushed into the swamp. After the revived Ronnie settled down again, Junior gave up the chase. Then, we all began to look for Earl. Midnight came and went before we could convince him to leave the swamp.

We were never again able to duplicate the thrill of "The Massacre at Coon Hill." Earl never really forgave us for our invasion of his innocent imagination. I can understand why. And, I can understand why Junior is a successful insurance salesman.

§§§§§§

THERMODYNAMICS...THE HARD WAY

I come from Chumuckla, Florida (a place that is closer to LeFlore, Mississippi—in land miles and in the nature of the land and its people—than it is to Tampa, Florida).

17

In Chumuckla we learned about physics early in life. It was not the stuff about quantum theory and black holes. It was of a more practical nature. My first lesson, as I remember it, focused on the theory of "Thermodynamics," or the transfer of heat.

In 1957 my big brother and I were second and third graders at Chumuckla School. Jim and I commuted by bus. "Number 53" came by our farm every weekday, grinding gears and belching blue smoke. Some days we waited over half an hour for "Ol' Man" Claude Jernigan to get to our stop with the bouncing yellow box on wheels. In the wintertime, the temperature often dropped to a toe-freezing liver-congealing cold. As native Floridians, we knew we did not have to own a coat—let alone wear one. It was our privilege.

But the northern state of Alabama refused to cooperate. Frequently, a blast of frigid Alabama air would slip, unannounced, 15 miles south of the border, where it would park right on top of our pink exposed ears. It was our preference to not wear a coat. To do so would be an admission of frailty. Never would we admit the need for a coat on a freezing day. My brother and I were much too tough. The lack of a coat, however, spurred creative thought and activity on our part.

In these conditions, as we waited for the warm, if noisy, shelter of the bus, we discovered what is known as "radiant" heat. The sun, you see, would pass heat energy to us along with the light energy—if we stood directly in its glow. The blacktop highway warmed up, stored the heat overnight, and radiated part of the energy back to the air above it.

At this point you have probably realized our discovery of "Prevost's Law." It mathematically describes radiant heat: $(Q/\lambda) - dA(t4 - tb4)$. Not long afterward, we discovered another formula: $Q - KA(t2 - t\gamma/d)\lambda$. As you know, this formula explains the theory of convective heat. Heat stored by the black-topped highway would pass directly to our goose-bump-infested skin merely by forcing direct contact between the two. So we decided to lie on the highway to absorb heat directly from the warm tar.

We did this for a couple of very cold mornings. If we saw a car top the hill or heard a car engine in the distance, we jumped up immediately and rushed off the road. Then our bare flesh cooled down again, a result of the "Alabama Arctic Air," and it was back to the road and convection heating.

It was a sensible approach to our problem. Developing motor skills and reflexes from dodging the cars was a bonus in our physical development—we felt! Learning about "thermodynamics" was an exciting discipline.

One morning, as she drove to school, my second grade teacher, Mrs. Whitley, saw Jim and me performing this practical application of physics. She, too, found the experience exhilarating. Jim and I could tell, because when she hit the brakes and skidded, her eyes were wide with excitement (and terror). She reported our brilliant discovery of "thermodynamic principles" to our parents that same day. After school, Momma explored the "thermodynamics" of applied friction with us. It was a lesson in practical physics that made a significant impression on our—*minds*.

Soon after the incident, Jim and I began to wear jackets. We even wore our jackets in moderately cool weather.

$$\oint\oint\oint\oint\oint\oint$$

THE PRACTICAL APPLICATION OF ELECTRICITY

We learned electrical engineering in the 10th grade at Chumuckla School. Part of our Vocational Agriculture curriculum, it was taught by Mr. Norman "Plug" Walther. Arc welding was our experimental medium.

The objective, of course, was to learn about electricity. But we were also to try constructing something of a useful nature that we could apply to the farming profession. My brother, Jim, constructed a most ingenious thing—a tractor lift. It was driven by the power lift of the tractor itself. It was a prodigious invention.

Jim applied the formula for leverage (T = f x l) to produce the contraption. When placed in commission, it lifted the entire back end of a Ford "red-belly" off the ground. The arrangement allowed us to swap both rear tractor tires from "inside configuration" to "outside configuration" with minimal effort. I never built anything so useful with my arc welding skills.

One day, it was my job to assist another welder. In my bare hands, I held the metal clamps that joined the steel parts together. The weld was moving along at a good pace. It is easy to tell when a welding job is being done properly. The sound made by the electric arc approximates that of a brown, grade B, medium hen's egg frying in a cast iron skillet in hot, day-old bacon grease.

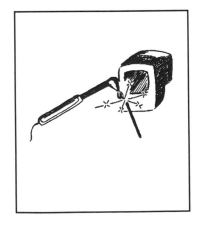

I stood on a thick rubber mat for insulation. However, early morning "Dixie Dew" covered the mat, canceling any insulating effect. I did not notice the dampness. My body was, in fact, an electrical ground conduction device for the arc welding machine.

When the shock came, it charged my body with enough electricity to perform the dance of a thousand battery-operated toy bears running on a parallel bank of two thousand "D-cell" "Neversaydie" super nickel-cadmium batteries. The electric jolt cured my acne problem for a week. The pain of the experience brought tears to my eyes.

One of the Enfinger boys teased me for being a cry-baby. With tears flowing down my now clear-complexioned cheeks, I let fly with a right hook and hit him squarely on the jaw. (I do not recommend this response...it hurts the hand worse than it hurts the target of your misspent emotion.) More tears followed as I realized from my bruised hand that I would never become a concert pianist.

And that's how I learned all I will ever need to know about electrical engineering.

§§§§§§§

THE FLORIDA STATE FAIR

The year was 1964. I was not educated in the world of complex physics. $E=mc^2$, black holes, and quarks were things I would not hear of for several more years. But our Vocational Agriculture teacher, Mr. Walther, was a determined educator. He started me and my fellow Future Farmers of America on the road to discovery.

"Plug" Walther packed seven juveniles into the school's green International Harvester pickup truck. The truck carried a drafty aluminum camper shell over its bed. It took all of us to Tampa, where we were expected to judge livestock in State competition. Each of us had about $25 to spend. We wore our blue and gold FFA jackets with the pride of gloried peacocks.

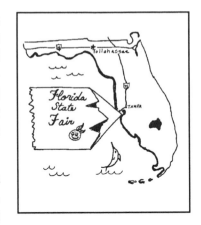

Some of us had never seen a building over ten stories tall. The old San Carlos Hotel in Pensacola was the tallest building within a hundred miles of Santa Rosa County. Our hotel in Tampa had nineteen floors.

My brother Jim, Eddie Kilcrease and his cousin Jimmy, and I climbed to the roof of the hotel, where we threw toilet tissue over the edge of the building, into the wind. The paper trailed through the twilight, wafting gently to the streets below. It was a majestic view.

We then tried heavier objects. Somebody dropped a rock. We carefully timed its descent as it sailed earthward and crashed into the pavement. We imagined ourselves as young Galileo Galileis researching the law of freely falling bodies.

Someone found a bolt lying loose on the roof (it wasn't me!). Now, we could execute a worthy experiment. Which falls faster, a rusty metal bolt or a roll of toilet tissue?

Oddly, it was not the law of gravity that brought our scientific research to a halt. It was an obscure and insidious law of physics called "The Coriolis Force." It states, in so many words, that an object in motion over the earth's surface will not necessarily fall where a fourteen year old believes it should, because the object isn't the only thing moving. The earth is turning underneath it as well. So both the object *and* the earth are in motion.

It seems the earth turned just enough to place the hotel restaurant skylight directly underneath the rapidly descending bolt. The sound of exploding glass signaled an end to our experiment.

I have as yet to explain, however, why the toilet paper fell through the hole exactly 2.3 seconds behind the bolt. My laboratory notes and mathematical calculations made at the time do not explain it. The question haunts me to this day. I hope to complete the experiment when I am not under the control of a strict legal guardian. (My wife thinks the idea is ludicrous.)

The culprit and all his laboratory assistants were quickly rounded up. In fact, "Plug" collared the entire livestock judging team, including Kenny Horton, Wayne White, and Jeff Bohannan. All of us experienced yet another lesson in thermodynamics by applied friction. "Plug's" genuine tanned cowhide S. S. Kresge belt left its warm impression.

The hotel staff cordially and singularly invited us to never again break bread with them or to grace their lobby with our presence.

I don't remember much about the "State Fair" except I saw one of the largest hogs I had ever seen or expect to see again. Those of us who were in Tampa that year, however, will tell you that our knowledge of "practical physics" was given a considerable boost for our having been there.

In the future, "Plug" would use greater discrimination in choosing the livestock judging teams that represented our school. They would be less scientifically inclined.

§§§§§§§

HIBISCUS ESCULENTUS

It was 1961. "Big Bucks" were a dream for my brother and me. I looked forward to the day when I could buy a whole dollar's worth of "Bazooka" bubble gum in one mad spending spree. Jim wanted a great deal more. He envisioned a time when he would purchase a genuine cedar box turkey call (guaranteed to faithfully reproduce the mating call of a young turkey hen) for only $4.95 plus shipping and handling. It was advertised in a four-year-old copy of "Field and Stream" magazine. Jim read the advertisement every time we visited Tom Moore's barber shop on Stewart Street in Milton.

Cannabis Sativa. America's number one cash crop. Money is made with it. The margin of profit is high. Repeat sales are a natural. An officer of the law once told me that, as a boy, he helped harvest the plant for the manufacture of hemp ropes. At the time, he was not told about the THC (tetrahydrocannabinol), the addictive chemical component. Now that he is in law enforcement, he wishes he had never heard of the plant. We never considered growing or selling the Cannabis plant for any number of reasons. We just said "NO."

Papaver Somniferum. This is another high-profit flower—seductively red and addictive to extremes. Seedlings were not available in our area. Neither Jay Feed and Seed nor Chaver's Farm Store in Milton could supply propagation materials. The "Burpee Spring Seed Catalog" had no listing for the plant. We never tapped its potential either.

In our quest for "Big Bucks," Cannabis was out. Papaver was out. We settled on an unusual flowering plant, Malvaceae Hibiscus esculentus. H. esculentus is closely related to Malvaceae Gossypium hirsutum—cotton, as it is called by most people. It is utilitarian in nature and carries none of the bold enchantments of its cousin. The cotton plant produces a unicellular, cellulosic carbohydrate polymer fiber with zero bioavailability. Its general formula is $C_6H_{10}O_5$, and it has a specific gravity of 1.54.

Hibiscus esculentus, on the other hand, carries mucilaginous polymerized fibrils within its seed vessel. These lend themselves to molecular restructuring when thermal energy is applied, thereby allowing rapid metabolic absorption within the body. The leaves are alternate, palmately lobed and veined with small deciduous stipules. The flowers are large, showy, and variously borne. Even a small crop of Hibiscus esculentus would be easy to spot from the air by trained observers. Covert propagation would be difficult.

The plant had its origins in Africa. There are many kinds of Hibiscus. This variety is particularly enchanting. One can imagine Queen Hatshepsut, in 1495 B.C., trafficking in the fruit of this plant. Egypt was a world power at the time—in part, I suspect, because of the influence of H. esculentus.

Presumably, the profitable slave trade practiced by traders from New England lent a hand in establishing this enticing plant on American soil. The slaves, realizing their dependency on it, smuggled valuable seeds to begin cultivation in the "New World." It thrived in the Gulf Coastal Plains. With time, the free population, as well, was caught in the alluring grip of the plant.

Amazingly, we grew it right under the noses of our parents. We did not do it alone either. I will name names. There were the Hatfield boys, Doug and Jerry; the Burch kid,

25

Tim; the brothers, Tony and Timmy Cook; the sisters, Edna and Betty Simmons with their brother, Charlie. Danny Ellis, Joe Cook, Mac Ryals, and Ray Kelly are also implicated. Often, the entire Longmire family of Milton would join us in the venture.

At 4 a.m. these people helped us harvest the valuable crop under cover of predawn darkness. We sold it on street corners in the clear sight of the law. Cash money and product would often change hands right at the curb.

Our business contacts in Pensacola and Milton used names like "James Manning," "Harland Johnson," "Marvin and Ethel Henderson," "Warner Urquhart," "Fred Brooks," "David Bailey," and "George Haber." All have respectable names in the *culinary* commerce of Escambia and Santa Rosa Counties.

I have described the power of this plant to some of my Northern acquaintances. They are curious about how to extract the greatest pleasure from it. Some want to know how to smoke it. Some express concern about the spread of disease should they inject the essence with a dirty needle.

"Can you snort the seeds?" I will not tell them, but it is more simple than that.

Unlike the THC of Cannabis (marijuana), or the opium and heroin from Papaver somniferum (the poppy), all you have to do with OKRA is boil it or fry it with corn meal. Better yet, Momma stir fries it with some onions and then she adds fresh sliced tomatoes.

Served with hot buttered cornbread, and fresh white field peas you will have the stuff dreams are made of!

§§§§§§

26

THE SEEDS OF RELIGION

Intent on creating land for cultivation on our farm, Pop pressed into service the energies and talents of his children—Jim, my sister Wanda, and me. The three of us were particularly well suited to the drudgery of clearing "new ground." We had two hands apiece. We were built low to the ground. And, we did not know any better.

We cleared five or ten acres every year until Pop felt he had enough arable land to farm. Or maybe it was until we were old enough and clever enough to figure out a way to avoid the work. I am not sure which came first.

When the rains held up progress and planting time drew critically near, Pop would hire healthy, innocent, unsuspecting kids from Milton. This was not the kind of work one volunteered for. He hired Thad Pace once; Thad caught on rather early. He never came back. David Bailly (Ed and Mary's boy) tried it for a spell; he quickly found "other employment." Mac Ryals came all the way from Detroit to earn the "fruits of labor." He eventually left the migrant labor pool and became a permanent resident.

Once cleared, the first crops to grow on the fresh earth would be watermelons, okra, squash, and cucumbers. Later, we would grow sweet corn. In years to follow, field corn or soybeans flourished. Pop told us his watermelon customers insisted on melons grown in "new ground." There were some who claimed taste sensitivity to the presence of ammonium nitrate. Artificial fertilizer was forbidden.

Watermelons required fresh, natural earth. There was no alternative. The first step was to clear the land. A bulldozer took out the big trees and pushed up the debris into long ragged rows. The remaining stumps, roots, and small trees were a job for potentially idle youth or convicts. There were no convicts available in Chumuckla.

I gazed at my first field full of roots, trees, and brambles. I knew the project required the miraculous help of God. I paused and began to meditate over this problem of labor—*my* labor. Pop quickly observed my lack of enthusiasm.

"Get out there in that field and start picking up roots, Boy. The Lord helps them that helps themselves," he bellowed.

"Pop," I explained, "All we need is the faith of a mustard seed. If we really believe, the Lord will move those roots."

Pop was quick to reply, "To try your faith worketh patience, and I ain't got much more patience!"

"He maketh me to lie down in green pastures (anything but a root patch)," I murmured. The test of religion, at that instant, reached a fevered pitch.

"Spare the rod and spoil the child," replied Pop. His face turned crimson with anger. The carotid artery that pulsates between the upper jaw and the lower ear began to tense with increasing pressure. His eyes grew to slits. His ears were pulled back close to his precision military haircut. Then, he cut a persimmon switch from a nearby tree.

It was in those next few moments that Pop explained religion to me in a way I have never more clearly felt or understood. I made a mental note for the future. I would try my very best to avoid religious arguments with Pop. By March, the land was cleared and ready for planting.

§§§§§§§

THE WRECK OF THE 1959

Eight pistons, roaring with the power of high-test gasoline, engine throbbing with power, drive shaft spinning, wheels turning.   There could be no greater thrill for a ten-year old.   To take Pop's new car for a spin, and feel the power in my hands.

No license to drive.   Didn't need one; not the way I saw it. I was on private property. There was plenty of room on the farm.   Driving looked easy from the passenger's seat. I had seen the folks shift gears a thousand times, and it was clearly simple to stomp (a) the accelerator (b) the clutch, or (c) the brake.

I had the facts down cold.   Unfortunately, theory is sometimes difficult to translate into practice.

I took the car without permission, before the folks were out of bed.   Figured I should have a private introduction to the new 1959 Ford Galaxy.

The introduction went well until the morning sun smeared a glare on the windshield.   The brake, the clutch, and the accelerator became a confused tangle.   When I lowered myself from my balanced perch on the steering wheel to see which pedal was where, a telephone pole jumped out and clipped the left fender.

It was only a small crunching sound.   Couldn't be bad, I thought.   When I finally got the machine returned to its proper place of rest and silenced the engine, I had a chance to see the damage.

Busted headlight; crunched fender; bent bumper. It was not a pretty sight—"the wreck of the 1959." As soon as Pop saw it, I knew it would make a grown man cry. Being of sound mind, my solution was simple: run away.

I went to the Davis house, where my buddy Donnie and I played horseshoes and hunted wild insects. Mrs. Davis fed both of us breakfast. Later I went with them to Jay, where Mr. Davis got a haircut. I was hoping the Davis family would adopt me, and I would never have to go home again. I figured my life in the Campbell family was over.

A phone call from home finally tracked me down. I thanked the Davises for all their kindness and went to face my fate. I was convinced it would be the end of the world, as I had come to know it.

I was surprised.

Mom and Pop explained to me that the "Wreck of the 1959" was bad, but it was better that I was O.K. Nevertheless, Pop explained, I would have to be punished for not facing up to my error in judgment. I was not punished for wrecking the car, but for not "facing the music."

Much later, after "The Wreck of the 1952" (an old Chevy pickup) and "The Wreck of the 1966," (a Ford Fairlane), I was glad I had learned the lesson early. The folks were much easier on me when I squarely faced the terms of my own predicaments.

Maybe there is a lesson in this somewhere.

$$\oint\oint\oint\oint\oint\oint\oint$$

THE DEATH OF OL' CRAZE...

Most of us experience the loss of a pet at some point in our lives. It is a virtual requirement in the curriculum leading to adulthood. No matter how attached we become to our beloved pet, we must inevitably face its demise. Hearts are broken. Tears are shed. Memories linger.

The first pet we lost was Davy. Davy was a bird, a parakeet. We named him after Davy Crockett. We taught him to say his name when we sang the "Davy Crockett" ballad from the Walt Disney movie.

"Born on a mountain top in Tennessee, killed him a bar when he was only three...," we sang. Davy would chime in with his name as if on cue.

Since he could only say "Davy" and he said it continuously, even without music, I am not entirely certain he was as brilliant as we thought.

We let him out of his cage one day. We wanted him to be a pioneer, like his namesake. He explored the living room. He "explored" on the couch, on the coffee table, and on the bookshelf. We rushed to get Davy back in his cage before he did any more exploring.

As we slammed the door to block his getaway, he flew into the doorway, meeting an untimely end. Davy died of a broken neck. The accident ended his singing career.

Davy had a proper burial. His coffin was a large matchbox (the kind kitchen matches come in). We made a small cross out of popsicle sticks and buried him near the honeysuckle vine in our back yard.

Thereafter, we had a regular procession of pets into our home—and out the back door. By the time we were grown, there was a rather large memorial park dedicated to their remains (and to their memory) in our back yard.

I was reminded of Davy when our friends the Bergs told us about the death of their dog, Craze.

Craze was a member of the family. He was a fourteen-year-old beagle. Craze was deaf, nearly blind, and almost completely lame. The family loved him immensely.

It was on a family outing to the lake when "Ol' Craze" passed on to the "Great Golden Kennel" in the sky. Craze was an avid swimmer—in his day. The lake excited what few senses remained within his feeble memory. When nobody was looking, the old dog eased himself into the shallow water and began to swim. "Ol' Craze" headed for deeper water, casually dog paddling along.

When the family saw him, he was already seventy-five yards out. They shouted in vain for his attention. The old beagle could not hear them. He could not see them either. "Ol' Craze" was in the only element left on earth that he could enjoy—and that, too, was about to end.

The children cried. The grandparents called out. Father Berg swam out to save "Ol' Craze." But the old dog ran out of energy. He gave up, and he drowned.

The youngsters were heartbroken. They sobbed all the way home. Mother Berg explained that Craze's time on earth was gone. Now he would go up to heaven.

That sad evening, following the prescribed ritual, Craze was buried in a cardboard box in the back yard. Each member of the family said a final kind word over the grave. They all turned to go in the house. That is, all except Junior Berg.

The four-year old, concern on his face, spoke up in protest. "Mommy, we can't go in yet. We gotta watch him go to Heaven!"

The dutiful parents sat down with the boy. Eye to eye, they gently explained, as best they could, the concepts of life and death, heaven and earth. When their infinite wisdom was spilled completely out, a look of understanding came over the boy's face.

"Now I understand," he said. "But, will the box go up there too?"

$$\oint\oint\oint\oint\oint\oint$$

THE BUBBLE GUM GENERATION GROWS UP

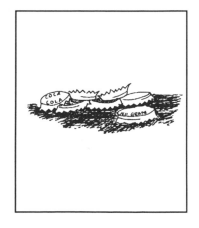

The Chumuckla High Class of '67 will hold its 20-year reunion next year (1987). I missed the 10-year reunion. I heard thirty-five percent of the class showed up—six people. We were a class of 17—unusually large for Chumuckla.

A revolution has taken place in our society over the short span of 20 years. Not all the changes are for the better.

When compared with the youth of my generation, young people today are spoiled. For instance, in the old days, there were only two brands of bubble gum, "Double Bubble" and "Bazooka." "Double Bubble" had the best comics, but the "Bazooka" tasted better. "Bazooka" had a full-bodied, fruity bouquet. It carried a suggestion of impetuousness. There was a hint of excitement. A mere whisper of fine powdered sugar covered this pink miracle of processed sapodilla tree extract (chicle). It was irresistible.

When "Double Bubble" started marketing a chunk style and then dropped the comics, "Bazooka" had a field day. At least for my money, they did.

Compare the choices today—an unlimited assortment of wimpy brand names to spoil the kids. "Bubble-icious," "Bubble Yum," and "Chewels" are each available in a dozen unnatural flavors. They have 'mass advertised' their way into a soft generation. It is not easy to find natural-flavored "Double Bubble" or "Bazooka" any more. Most newer brands have removed all traces of sugar. Wherefore is it then, the "little people" will find the lesson of tooth decay?

In my day there was genuine "Coca-Cola." The real REAL THING. It was made with authentic sugar (sucrose). It was sold in six-ounce glass bottles. I could find it under about four and three-quarter inches of ice in the red "Coke" box at Pug Carnley's Grocery and Gulf Station in Chumuckla. The elixir was nearly frozen; a cold, mysterious vapor floated out of the opened bottle.

The "secret ingredient" was pure battery acid from indelicately aged pulpwood trucks. Of this I am ninety-nine percent positive. The "REAL Coke" could burn the hair off your tonsils. Paul Stewart, Chumuckla High Class of '67, Vietnam Veteran, Experienced Farmer ("Former Farmer"—same thing), and "TI" (Tough Individual) chugged two in rapid succession one summer day in 1965 at Bernie Diamond's Grocery Store and Standard Oil Company Gas Station in Brownsdale. Junior Wade was a witness. Paul's "near-death experience" inspired Junior to plan a career in the life insurance business. The last time I saw Paul, there was very little hair remaining on his head. Some people blame the loss of hair on genetics. Some blame the war. Some attribute the bald condition to farming. The truth is, it was those two six-ounce Cokes!

« »

Country stores did not have asphalt parking lots. The parking area was paved with flattened bottle caps, the result of a millennium of cola sales.

Bottles were used over and over again. Original bottling locations were stamped on the bottom of the bottle. We wagered a round of "Cokes" over the imprint. The loser held the bottle with the closest point of origin to Chumuckla. For instance, a bottle from Pocatello, Idaho, would easily win over one from Jackson, Tennessee. For many Americans, this would be their only contact with the study of geography. I don't know how youngsters learn geography today.

The modern "Coke" is sweetened with corn sugar (fructose). The caffeine level has been cut so low an addict might need a 55-gallon drum fed intravenously to ward off sleep. Even this may be too little to keep a caffeine devotee awake in a room full of dead people. They persist in saying it is the 'real thing,' but my doubts remain. Some colas have no caffeine at all—and no sugar either. They actually advertise the fact.

Six-ounce bottles are gone. Wooden bottle crates can only be found in antique stores.

« »

Good music aired from virtually any rock channel on the radio, 20 years ago. We had The Beatles, The Rolling Stones, The Birds, Canned Heat, Tiny Tim, and The Grateful Dead. Now, the artistic offering is garbage: Prince, Multiple Contusions, Kiss, Twisted Sister, Black Sabbath, Boy George, Banana Rama, and The Grateful Dead (they won't die). Weird names. Weirdo people. Weird-to-the-MAX music. What happened to sensible groups with meaningful names, like "Three Dog Night"?

« »

Buffalo Bob and Howdy Doody gave my generation solid role models. It was not long before Captain Kangaroo pushed Howdy aside. Then, network competition brought us Mister "nauseatingly nice" Rogers! Soon, Sesame Street arrived with certified education from a Big Bird. Is it proper for children to learn table manners from a Cookie Monster? I am saddened to report the younger set today believes "Howdy Doody" is a cryptic greeting between older people.

The first Baby Boomers are now 40 years old. The crop of 1949 is not far behind. I am no longer 24 years old. My belly is no longer flat. Years of vitamin therapy, a careful diet of cheeseburgers (no ketchup, extra onions), and (very) modest exercise has allowed my body to delicately age toward something a little less than perfection. I have aged more delicately than some of my contemporaries, but aged nonetheless.

In a recent cold spell, I wore a cardigan sweater to work. My mirror had not prepared me for the revelation that soon followed. Alas, a chance encounter one day with Patti, a young lady in our office, left a permanent mark on my ego.

Certainly, child labor laws are trampled underfoot when 19-year-old infants, like Patti, are hired to work in REAL jobs. She took note of my gray sweater, with its buttons and pockets. The corporate lass, a product of television education and a soft society, blurted, "Mister Campbell, you look like Mister Rogers!"

"Mister RAMBO Rogers to you, kid!"

$$\oint\oint\oint\oint\oint\oint$$

A FREE HAIRCUT FROM UNCLE BOBBY

Nowadays, we don't visit the barber shop to have surgery or to have a tooth pulled. In days gone by, however, that was the reason for barbers. A barber in the Fifteenth Century was likely to provide bloodletting and tooth-pulling services.

It was Henry VIII who separated the professions. Perhaps he was forced to make the ruling after his wife, Anne Boleyn, underwent radical hair surgery (beheaded at his own request). Those who now practice the tonsorial arts are a discipline apart from those who pull teeth, or who intentionally extract blood.

A few reminders of the surgical side of "barbery," are the red and white spiral striped pole and the surgically sharp razor. The pole is a symbol of bandages used by the barber of old after a bloodletting session.

Today there are different reasons to visit the barber shop. In the early part of the second half of this century, Pop took me to the barber shop. He insisted that I appear as normal as any other juvenile in our county. Crewcuts seemed to go well with buck teeth in that generation. In the 1960s, those who visited a barber shop were keenly interested in distancing their image from those who rebelled against both social order and old magazines.

I frequented Tom Moore's shop on Stewart Street in Milton. If Mr. Moore did not cut my hair, Mr. Schultz did. Mr. Schultz was deaf and speechless as well. I would point to the familiar poster on the wall, to show which hair style I preferred. If he thought Pop would approve, he gave it to me (I think).

The barber shops I frequented would have a healthy supply of old comic books. And behind the "Field and Stream" magazines was an adequate supply of WWII veterans. These men would occasionally offer one or another of several political observations for public consumption.

Sometimes I would visit Roy Barnhill, in Pace, for a haircut. Occasionally, I would visit Red Hudson's Barber Shop in Jay or Mr. Hinote's shop in Milton. Cletis Smith cut hair in Chumuckla for a time, but there was too little business and the shop closed. Each barber used about the same technique. Only the selection of magazines was different. I could read "The Farm Journal" in Red's, "Look" magazine at Roy's, and "National Rifleman" at Cletis's. "True Detective" magazines dating back to 1942 were in stock at Mr. Hinote's shop.

When I came home from the Navy, the first thing Pop did was take me with him to Jay. There, I was given a "regulation" haircut by Red Hudson. It was as if the Navy was not conservative enough, and Pop felt an obligation to reinstill the parochial values of the real world.

A barbershop is a good place to study local politics. My Uncle, Bobby Carswell, at the Marina Barber Shop in Panama City is a prime example. His shop continually hosts political leaders in the Bay County area. His advice and the counsel of his patronage are sought by both the meek and the powerful in State government.

When I visited Uncle Bobby, I could get a free haircut. The Governor, however, would have to pay. These days, I expect, most politicians are grateful the barber's art no longer includes bloodletting.

$$\oint\oint\oint\oint\oint\oint\oint$$

HOW TO MEET GIRLS...1904

In 1904, Chumuckla was a "*sub*burg." It is not a burg even today, although there is a modern, air-conditioned convenience store posted at the crossroads. The community is located directly across the Escambia River from Bogia, Florida. In 1904 it was not a shadow of the modern village it is today.

There were no paved roads. There was no central air conditioning. There were no Toyota pickup trucks with four-wheel drive, four-cylinder overhead cam engines. There were no AM/FM quadraphonic radios with compact laser disc players.

There was no electricity. I am told my ancestors had to watch black and white TV (with manual channel selectors) by candle light.

In that year, my Great Uncle Cuyler Campbell, a son of pioneers, had seen 15 Northwest Florida winters come and go. He witnessed the seasons change without the heartbreak of psoriasis or hypertension. He did not have a daily ration of Cocoa Puffs and Fruit Loops (prize in box).

At 98, Uncle Cuyler was a human library of the times. Not too long ago, he shared some of his early experiences with me.

In 1904 he and his brother (my Grandfather, Jim Campbell) reached an appropriate age to date. They owned some fine horses and they had a sporting buggy. They instinctively sought the company of young ladies who lived in distant communities. Jim and Cuyler (Grandpa and Great Uncle) wanted to practice the art of courtship.

In those days, it was not unusual to travel 25 miles in search of a good family. Respectable families usually had among their number a supply of suitable maidens. In Mulat, near Escambia Bay, they found twin sisters who met their stringent qualifications. They were Minnie and Mae Brown.

For some months, on Saturday afternoons following their introduction, Jim and Cuyler drove a team of horses to Mulat. Their matched team pulled a standout rig for twenty miles to the Brown family home.

They joined the family for dinner and then they would sit for a spell. About 8 o'clock in the evening they hitched up the buggy and headed for home in the dark. Sealed, quartz-beam headlights were not in use at that time.

Eventually, my Grandpa found another lass to court at the Howell homestead. The Howell family was closer—some five or six miles north of the Campbell farm. For a time, my Uncle Cuyler made the trip to Mulat alone.

It was not uncommon for him to fall asleep at the reins. It was late, he was relaxed with a soul full of good food and conversation. The horses, operating on an early version of

automatic pilot, found the way home without human inter-
vention. The roads were unpaved and unmarked. They
would remain so for another twenty or twenty-five years.

Once, according to Uncle Cuyler, the night was so still and
so dark the horses lost their way. Cuyler was awakened from
his gentle, rocking nap by an unusual bump. He strained his
eyes for a familiar landmark. There was none. He was lost.
Cuyler reined in the horses. He unhitched the buggy, and the
trio camped out on the spot. With daylight he would find his
way home.

As it turned out, he was somewhere near Pond Creek, off
course by six or seven miles, perhaps on what is today known
as Hamilton Bridge Road. Two wars later, there would be a
U.S. Navy practice landing field for student aviators in the
area—"Spencer Field." Of course, in 1904, nobody in Santa
Rosa County would have dreamed of such a thing.

The twenty-mile courtship was an effort. Maintaining the
horses was a job. I am sure he was disappointed when the
Brown girl turned her attentions toward a young man named
Jones. It was several years later before Cuyler's determined
efforts at courtship won him the hand of Bessie Savelle.

My wife, Karen (Gatewood) is a great-grand niece of the
Brown twins, whom my Great Uncle and Grandfather dated
near the turn of the century. Karen's Great Grandma Tinsley
was sister to the Brown twins, Minnie and Mae. Ed Tinsley
and Ed's sister, Floress Burnett, who still live in Avalon
Beach, are descendents of the Brown family.

Uncle Cuyler told me "You did well to marry into that
family, boy." I agreed.

Karen's Grandmother, Floress Burnett, remembers the
events mentioned here. She lost track of Uncle Cuyler and
my Grandfather shortly after they turned their attentions in

41

other directions. She was relieved to hear, after more than 80 years, that everything worked out so well for my Uncle.

My cousins—Clayton, Otto, Oswald, Evelyn , Lucille, Donald, Louise, Rufus, Glen, Winston, and Colbert—are also pleased with the turn of events. They are the offspring of Cuyler and Bessie. If relationships had developed otherwise, they might carry names like "A.G.," Leroy, Robert, May Evelyn (actual Jones descendents), Bertha, Ralph, Minerva, Arthur, Zebadiah, Calvin, and Theodore (or some such combination). And they would not look a bit like they do now.

$$\oint\oint\oint\oint\oint\oint$$

EAU DE HOOF...

In some ways, little has changed in Chumuckla over the last 80 years. Chumuckla is a community of farmers and other souls struggling with mortgages, low pay, little recognition, and poor television reception. It is a microcosm of the Twentieth Century "Dixie Experience."

The last story told how my Great Uncle Cuyler Campbell sought and courted young, respectable, ladies. He traveled to distant communities within Santa Rosa County. In 1904 his travel was restricted to horse-drawn wagons over unpaved roads, through rough terrain, and in all manner of weather. Even with all the effort to overcome the inconveniences of pioneer Florida, he was rejected by at least one prospective flower. In truth, he was probably turned down by several before he won the hand of Miss Savelle.

Move your calendar up sixty years. Flip the pages past "The Somme," "The Crash of 1929," "The Great Depression," "Pearl Harbor," "VJ Day," "Inchon," "I Like Ike," and "The Annual Chumuckla FFA/FHA Banquet of 1962" (Mabel Salter presiding). Turn the pages of your calendar all the way to about 1965. Look at a vision of the past.

There goes Cuyler's fifteen-year-old grand-nephew, Vic. He is wearing one of his best flannel shirts. He is riding his quarterhorse mare, Ol' Ripple. Vic is headed south alongside County Road 197 to visit and to impress the most recent passion of his heart, "The Little Jernigan Girl."

The roads have been paved now for some twenty or twenty-five years. White dotted lines were added to the blacktop, reducing the possibility of becoming lost. If ever in doubt, you can follow the dotted line back the way you came.

At the Jernigan home, Vic dismounts. He wipes some of the sweat off the horse and onto his shirt. He ambles to the front door. The walk is practiced to appear confident. The stride is somewhere between John Wayne and Roy Rogers.

He knocks politely, scrapes some manure off his brogan lace-up work boots, and is invited inside. Mrs. Jernigan is breathing shallow, but the boy does not know why. Maybe she is sick, he thinks. His "atmosphere" follows him to a chair. He removes his hat with a flair. The $2.97 straw hat is essential equipment for horseback riding. Boy Vic sits a spell with the family.

After some months of this modest approach, Boy Vic has a sixteenth birthday. He becomes an amazingly mature person. He claims—as his own—wisdom, confidence, common sense, and other mature characteristics.

On occasion, Pop loans Vic the 1965 blue, longbed, step-side, standard-transmission, Ford pickup truck. It has an excellent platform for dating girls. Clean out the hog manure from the last trip to the sale barn, and the smell is acceptable.

Enter Vic's buddy, Junior, who takes an interest in the dark-haired vixen. He enters the competitive field of contenders who vie for the attention of Miss Jernigan. With full battle gear—a two-tone, blue and white, 1965 Ford Galaxie (with a 390-cubic inch V-8 engine, automatic transmission, AM/FM radio, and air conditioning); a quart of Clubman aftershave; a Gant madras shirt; a pair of penny loafers with argyle socks; and a complete collection of Pete Fountain's LP Jazz albums, Junior turns her dark eyes from mine to his. Face the facts. "Kid Vic" is outgunned.

Junior held her attention for only a few months. He, too, was then abandoned for a more mature and better prepared gladiator.

Recall the last chapter—the story of Uncle Cuyler. I learned from my experience, much as he had 60 years before. First, we had to face the truth. Our magnetic personalities, good looks, fine manners, and almost irresistible charm would simply not move some women. There are rare exceptions where being very nearly perfect in almost every way is not a sufficient draw. Second, after careful analysis, it became obvious. The fault lay not with ourselves. The blame could be leveled at the horses.

A few hours ON horseback, or even IN a buggy BEHIND a horse, will lend a "certain aire" to the participating equestrian. It follows, logically, that this "aroma" or "eau de hoof" may not be altogether attractive to the sensitivities of refined ladies. Anyway, I noticed that my luck improved when I started dating with the pickup truck. My luck was even better when, in time, a car was available.

Barring the use of deodorant, the switch from horse to car had probably the most dramatic effect on my relationships with the fair gender. I am sure Uncle Cuyler, as well, had better results when he began courting from an automobile—of course, in 1904, the supply of autos was limited.

§§§§§§§

II

The Military and Me

"I do not wish to have command of any ship that does not sail fast, for I intend to go in harm's way."

John Paul Jones

"War is much too serious a thing to be left to military men."

Charles Maurice DeTalleyrand-Perigord

OCS WAS NO PICNIC

Newport, Rhode Island, is a picturesque New England town. It is an old seaport and a summer playground for the rich. The summer "cottages" of people like the Vanderbilts and the Bouvier (as in Jacqueline Onassis) are there. Yachting is a summer pastime for them.

Newport is also the home of Officer Candidate School for surface Naval officers. The OCS for air Naval officers is in Pensacola. My cousin, Officer Candidate Gainer, from Chipley, is in Newport (1989)—enjoying the invigorating climate and learning the "right way" to do things—the Navy way.

The surface Navy, as you may know, is a completely different animal from the air Navy. For instance, the air Navy will not allow its officers to carry parrots around on their shoulders. And they do not pay the crew with pieces of eight. All in all, the air Navy is not nearly as exciting as the surface Navy.

But Navy OCS is bad news for any poor soul—be it in Pensacola or in Newport. I remember it well. I am a graduate of that institution (barely). In the summer of 1970, I found myself in this place I learned to hate—OCS.

The poor Officer Candidates get up at 4:30 a.m. every day and run for two miles. Then they are allowed five minutes to shower, suit up, and report for breakfast, which lasts for at least another five minutes. Somebody is assigned the job of yelling at these bedraggled candidates for interminable periods of time. If the "yeller" can find a way to frustrate them and

47

make them feel as if their I.Q. is three points less than a rock, he will do it.

My cousin has a sense of humor, which is good. But OCS is a place so bereft of humor that a person with normal hormonal humor levels will approach death in a matter of hours. A recent letter from my cousin confirmed the worst: OCS has not changed.

Officer Candidate Gainer reports that "Q-Tips" are ideal for cleaning out window tracks. Life will never be the same unless the garbage can is exactly four inches from the radiator. Polishing shoes becomes second nature. A qualified Officer Candidate can strip a shoe down blindfolded, polish it, and relace it with only one hand. The Communists had better think twice before they invade!

Besides all the harassment, Officer Candidates attend school eight hours a day, learning things like navigation, engineering, fire fighting, radio and signal flag communications, and relative motion.

I never did get relative motion down: If the wind is blowing 15 knots at 063 degrees, the bogie is on course 254 (bearing 171 degrees), and the combined populations of India and China equal that of the rest of the world, what is the current speed and heading of your vessel?

I'm glad they made me a communications officer. At least I had turned on a radio before.

In November my cousin will begin her career as a Naval Officer. She will be a good one. And, when Stephanie has a chance to breathe, I hope she will take a look at the beautiful scenery of New England.

Of course, I am no longer in the Navy. It was a brief career for me. A few years of taking orders was all I could stand.

I have to go now. My wife wants me to take out the trash, vacuum the carpet, and clean the bathroom.

$$\$\$\$\$\$\$\$$

KAWASAKI, SEÑOR...

I studied English as a second language in high school. It was a requirement for graduation in those days. My native language is "Dixie," of course. My English teacher in high school, Mrs. Louise Driggers, faced an enormous challenge.

"Duh rayn en Spuhayne fawls muhainly own du puhlayn." We said it over and over again.

Occasionally, I have an opportunity to speak English with a true Brit, but it is a rarity. I have a good friend, Charlie, who is a Scot. He can't speak English well at all. Another friend, Lloyd, is Australian, and he speaks "Aussie"—not English.

"G'die Mite (Good day, mate)," says Lloyd.

I now work with a German company (1985), and many of my friends are, of course, German. Most of them speak excellent English, but it (English) is still a difficult language for me. Working with a German company in New Jersey creates a unique set of problems. The Germans speak English, the Yankees speak "Joisey," and I speak "Dixie."

A Jerseyan might say, "Let's go wark the dwag in the park." (Let's go walk the dog in the park.)

A Southerner might say, "Let's git duh dawgs and go fishin or sumpin." (Let's get the dogs and go fishing or something.)

"Sprechen Sie Deutsche?" (Do you speak German?), ask the Germans.

"Nein, Ich spreche 'Dixie'," (No, I speak Dixie), I reply.

In 1973 I was involved in a multinational naval exercise in the Pacific. My ship, the destroyer USS O'Callahan, issued fleet formation directions to destroyers from Australia, New Zealand, and Canada. I was the communications officer and spoke the captain's commands over the radio.

"Formashun tern bairing tooh seavuhn zeerow dugreez and foam a lahn abreaust."

The New Zealanders complained loudly over the radio that they could not understand my version of English. "Sigh agayne mite, owvir," (Say again, mate, over) they said. "We can't understand you Yanks.

I quickly informed them that I was no Yankee. I repeated the command several times, but they never got it right, and they would not turn until they did.

The Canadians turned the wrong way, and the Australians simply waited to see what we did. We needed an interpreter, or at the very least a common language.

It was when Lloyd, my friend from Tasmania, Australia, visited us a few years back that I hit upon the new universal language. I now find that I can converse with people of any nation simply by employing the "new standard."

"Kawasaki, Lloyd San," I said. "Oh! Honda!" he replied.

"Pana-sonic, akai, so-ny," I offered. "Seiko, fuji, nikon a subaru," he answered.

"Honda! Hai! Hai Haibachi, sansui toy-ota," I countered.

"Toyota?"

"You got it, Toyota."

So, for an upcoming business trip to Germany, I feel well prepared. I speak very poor German and not so good English. But everybody understands the "universal language" of Japan. "Ah so."

$$\oint\oint\oint\oint\oint\oint\oint$$

WE FOUND THE ENEMY...AND HE WAS US...

Soldiers and sailors throughout the land struggled to reach their units.

Crowds pressed them and jostled them in large cities and small towns. Sometimes people spit on them. Sometimes people threw rocks. It was common to receive an unkind, vulgar gesture from the natives. In some areas, they were simply shunned. People pretended they did not exist.

The uniforms were a dead giveaway. These soldiers were tools of U.S. military imperialism. They were not welcome. The times were troublesome. It was a dangerous country for American servicemen.

In peril, the young soldiers and sailors pressed on to join up with their comrades.

Some anticipated the hostilities. They camouflaged their appearance with civilian attire. They hoped to blend in with the nation's populace. Often as not, civilian clothes were merely a temporary ruse; the short hair, the innocent youth, and the green sea-bags were telltale identification. They were marked military targets.

Small battles took place. One-on-one encounters between an intellectual pacifist and the kid in uniform. The intellectual, who was probably a student of defunct world cultures returning to school after a weekend of revelry, sincerely tried to spark the ideal of pacifism in the young gladiator's heart.

Self-anointed moralists chastised the evil sailor, who was armed only with a comb, a cigarette lighter, dog tags, and his heavy (very heavy) sea-bag. " Warmonger!"

In crowded transportation terminals, the boy soldier was accosted by young religious devotees clothed in saffron robes. The youthful saffron inductees lectured the innocent military inductee about the evils of war. They asked for a donation to help the cause of peace. The soldier donated a dime. Later, another tribe espoused world peace. He donated a nickel. By the third time the poor soldier was asked for a donation to promote universal peace, his vote came down decidedly in favor of war.

Were it not for a generally silent but sympathetic underground network of people who cared, many American soldiers and sailors might have been lost before they could rejoin their units.

This was America in 1972.

I recall the summer of 1972. The USS O'Callahan crew returned to their ship. Sailors rebounded from their final shore leave. One pink seaman apprentice, with a smattering of adolescent whiskers standing defiantly at attention between the mountainous pimples on his cheeks, marched aboard with a Bible under his arm. It was newly purchased from a street vendor hawking the imitation leather-bound Book. The sailor had paid an extra twenty dollars to have his mother's name embossed on the cover in imitation gold. Others struggled aboard with the odor of a distillery clinging to the air about them.

The captain ordered the bow line cast off. He ordered the engine back one third. The ship's horn sounded one long blast, followed by three short blasts. We backed into the San Diego Harbor.

The O'Callahan steamed past Point Loma and made for open sea. Most were apprehensive, but the apprehension was tempered with a sense of adventure. We steamed west to join the 7th Fleet and do battle with an enemy. It felt good to be among our own kind, having passed through a nation of hostile strangers.

It was an odd time to be in uniform.

Years have healed the animosity among fellow Americans in those times. Today, there is a healthy respect for people in uniform.

That is as it should be.

$$\oint\oint\oint\oint\oint\oint\oint$$

ALL IS QUIET NOW...

New Year's Day, 1973. A cease fire. A small task group of destroyers and frigates was assigned to shore bombardment in the DMZ area of Vietnam. It was a quiet but busy time.

The USS O'Callahan was in the company of the destroyers Morton, Rupertus, Hollister, Tucker, Blandy, and Wiltsie. Their five-inch gun barrels were blackened from action. They were peeling paint. All made use of the quiet time to re-arm and refuel.

Mr. Kissinger would sign an agreement with Le Duc Tho a few weeks later. When that happened the United States would end its direct involvement in the tragic war. The news was full of talk about negotiations. We anticipated some kind of ending very soon.

Meanwhile, the forces remaining in combat were to put as much pressure on their adversaries as possible. Our objectives were to force North Vietnam to sit in negotiations. We were also to impress South Vietnam with our unswerving allegiance to their cause. It seemed neither objective was being met.

On New Year's Eve, the Hollister was riddled with shrapnel. It ventured within range of what appeared to be a 105-mm enemy battery deployed on a hill overlooking the DMZ and the Gulf of Tonkin. I watched the Hollister's punishment with my shipmates from a few miles away.

I have imagined a North Vietnamese officer in charge of that gun. I've envisioned him dressed in a muddy uniform with a rotting pith helmet atop his head. He was probably barefoot. The sighting and ranging device for his artillery piece was probably a half circle of sticks in the mud, a few yards out from his position. A second stick nearer to him would line up with one of the sticks in the half circle. Firing positions could be plotted from this arrangement. When a ship ventured in range and fell in line with his sticks, he would merely swing the gun to a predetermined angle and let loose a barrage of fire.

Of course, our weapons systems were more sophisticated. Our group commander aboard the Morton was determined to teach this enemy artilleryman something about American technology. He made plans with the Blandy to approach the beach as soon as the cease fire lifted. They would "smoke out" the culprit—tempt him to expose his position. Plans were discussed over a secure radiotelephone. Those of us who could understand the "Donald Duck" talk (voices scrambled and descrambled over the "RED PHONE") were privy to the plan.

The Blandy's plan was to approach the beach with The Morton "riding shotgun" a few hundred yards astern, off the port quarter. The Blandy would draw the fire from our adversary. All hands aboard both ships would scour the mountains with high-powered binoculars, infrared sensors, fire control radar, and various electronic wonders. When The Blandy came under fire, The Morton would pinpoint the flash and "nail the sucker" with computer-controlled rapid-fire, five-inch/fifty four naval guns.

Air support was never considered. Any destroyer sailor will tell you the Naval Air Corps is simply not effective in combat. Besides, this was a job for the "Real Navy."

The cease fire was lifted at 1800 hours. The Blandy approached the coast, steaming at four knots. The slow speed allowed for accurate computer-generated target data. The Morton was close behind. They came in range—sleek, grey, computerized machines of destruction, built to go in harm's way.

55

Splash, splash, splash, splash, and more splashes!!!

Both The Blandy and The Morton were covered with spray from the enemy artillery fire exploding in the sea around them. Neither ship fired an effective round. Gunsmoke covered the gulf waters. For a moment, the heart-stopping scene was totally obscured by the smoke and spray. Both ships turned on their heels and raced for the open sea as fast as their engine order telegraphs could ring up "FLANK SPEED."

So much for technology.

§§§§§§§

COUNTERBATTERY

"We have a loud explosion on the port side of the engine room," reports the Engineering Officer, Ensign Morano.

Even as I hear his voice over the sound-powered phones on the bridge, Ensign Shanline orders the helm to come about, 180 degrees: Steady on course 080. The rudder is right— 35 degrees.

Spray from a shell splashing not 50 yards off the port bow is already turning to a fine mist and a permanent memory.

Ensign Shanline commands the engine order telegraph to full speed. The ship responds and heels to starboard, making a sharp turn. We gain speed, increasing from four knots to twenty-five knots in seconds that drag on for hours. The ship's turbines scream loudly as the 1200-psi boilers make steam to turn them.

Another explosion is reported overhead by Signalman Second Class Talamante. He is in the signal shack above the bridge. Ensign Machino, in the fire control radar cockpit over our heads, ducks—as though the six inches he can move will protect him—and reports the same explosion.

Ensign Shanline has the "Conn" this night. My job is that of Bridge Communications Officer. I report the Captain's orders to fire over the sound-powered phones. I feed internal communications of the ship back to the Captain. The ship's captain is Commander Dunham.

Our mission: Coastal bombardment; nighttime harassment; interdiction of enemy activity (H&I in military shorthand). Our position is "Point Allison, Station Papa." Four other destroyers are strung out along the coast, separated by about two miles.

These are the last days of the Vietnam War. South Vietnamese Marines have established a beachhead at the mouth of the Cua-Viet River, near the DMZ. They need the protection afforded by seaborne firepower.

We steam a track diagonal to the coast. Computers and navigation aides in Combat Information Center (CIC) plot the next target. Our speed is necessarily slow for accurate target data generation. To avoid unnecessary illumination of our own position, we use flashless powder in our five-inch guns. However, when The O'Callahan approaches within one mile of the coast, with a clear sky and a brilliant full moon, it becomes a target of unrestricted opportunity.

Ensign Shanline responds as soon as the first enemy shell splashes. A monotone, businesslike conversation develops between me and the others connected to the phone system throughout the ship. In seconds a story emerges. Damage control teams mobilize. Guns shift targets to seek out a more pressing challenge, and months of training condense into pure "essence of Navy." It tastes like a lifetime.

"Bridge..CIC," says Ensign Dave Grimes, our assistant CIC Officer of the Watch. "Bridge Aye," I respond.

"Can you tell us where the shells are landing?" "We have one splash fifty yards off the port bow."

"Are there more?"

"Wait one"...(silence).

"Bridge, Engine Room." "Bridge, aye."

"We have a loud explosion on the port side of the engine room." "Damage Control...Bridge, report to the Engine Room." "Damage Control, aye."

"CIC...Bridge, Engine Room reports an explosion on the port side." "Bridge...CIC, any more reports?"

"Wait one."

"Bridge...Signal." "Bridge, aye."

"Signal...Bridge reports an explosion overhead."

"CIC...Bridge, one explosion reported overhead."

"Bridge...CIC, any more reports?"

"Wait one."

"Gun Control, Bridge."

"Gun Control, aye."

"Stand by to fire five salvos, flashless, H.E. (high explosive), after gun mount, target number four three, range...

("Nine thousand two hundred yards," said a voice)...nine thousand two hundred yards...at my command." (Only the captain gives the orders to shoot.) The location of the counterbattery was a guess. We could not see the enemy guns.

The Captain commanded, "Shoot."

"Shoot," I repeated the order, speaking to Gun Control, deep in the bowels of the ship. The gunners mate pulled the trigger on a computerized handgun facsimile with a wooden pistol grip.

Five angry salvos responded to the enemy counterbattery. It was surely not an accurate response, but it was at least an answer in kind.

"CIC...Bridge, after lookout reports a splash one hundred yards off the stern."

The O'Callahan moved out of range.

"All stations...Bridge, report damage and casualties."

By now there was a "less-romantic" distance between our ship and the enemy gunners. The USS O'Callahan had sustained a glancing hit on the port side near the Engine Room. Some shrapnel sparked across the open signal bridge. There were no casualties.

We never saw the enemy coastal battery. CIC tried to plot the fall of shells. They hoped perhaps to correlate the splash points with a direction of fire. They were not successful.

Similar actions were repeated with The O'Callahan and with other ships on the "gunline" in those last days of the Vietnam War. Most passed through these periodic shell showers with minimal or no damage.

The South Vietnamese Marines courageously held their beachhead until the official U.S. cease fire was declared on January 27, 1973. But their heroic stand was doomed.

American warships moved out to sea—twenty miles off the coast. There they stood by, passively observing the historic terms of the Paris Agreement. Marines pleaded for gunfire support over the radio. There was no response. The United States was, officially, no longer a part of the conflict.

Within days, the North Vietnamese Army overran the Marines and annihilated them.

$$\text{\$\$\$\$\$\$\$}$$

THE CHRISTMAS BOMBING...

Fellow anthropoids often try very hard to find something in common. When meeting strangers, we search for the thread of common experience or knowledge that will link them to our own small galaxy. People like other people better when they have something in common.

Not long ago, I visited the offices of one of my customers in Birmingham, Alabama. My business contact and friend was Steve Collier. I asked him to join me for lunch. With him was a fellow he introduced as Dave. I asked Dave to join us.

Dave is the corporate pilot.

"Where did you learn to fly, Dave?"

"Air Force," was the answer.

"Air Force," I repeated. "Too bad. Everybody knows the Navy has the best pilots."

"Some Navy pilots are O.K. I applied to both the Navy and the Air Force, but the Air Force offer came two weeks before the Navy bureaucracy could respond. Besides," he offered, "my wife, Mary, and our twin daughters, Karen and Kathryn, think Air Force pilots are the best."

"Sounds like a biased opinion to me. When were you in the Air Force?", I queried.

"From '69 through '74," says he.

"What sort of plane did you fly?"

"B-52."

"Well, at least you had eight engines. Navy pilots get only one engine, sometimes two....Dave, were you by any chance involved in the 'Christmas Bombing' of Hanoi in 1972?"

"Yes, I participated in the 'Linebacker Two' operation."

He spoke with precision. No word wasted. I guess pilots are like that. I explained to Dave and Steve that my ship, the Navy frigate O'Callahan, was in the area at the time. We were assigned to a search and rescue (SAR) station about 20 miles off Haiphong Harbor, in the Gulf of Tonkin. We were to wait for damaged aircraft that might ditch over the water.

We viewed the world from a circular green phosphorescent radar screen. I asked Dave about his "view from the top," so to speak.

Dave shared with us his experience. Steve and I paid rapt attention.

"The 'view from the top' on December 18 was not so good," said Dave. He had lost No. 7 engine to low oil pressure on the 3400-mile trip from Guam. There was an "undercast." The targets were not easy to see.

I remember this part clearly from the radar picture aboard ship. The planes were in a neat, WWII-style formation. I could see the leading dot (plane) on our scope placing a pattern of aluminum chaff ahead of the main formation. The chaff confused the enemy radar over Hanoi and helped in some ways to protect the bomber formation.

Dave continued. "Over Hanoi, the missiles attacked the bomber formation in salvos. This was not expected, because conventional tactical analysis would say this is a wasteful use of firepower by the enemy. The American bombers expected frugal use of missiles, supported by lots of antiaircraft flak."

"The enemy was not held by convention, however, and the massive, wholesale use of SA2 radar-controlled missiles could hardly miss finding a few B-52 bombers—if only by accident—in such a flock of aircraft."

There was a *bumper crop* of bombers for the North Vietnamese to harvest.

"The missiles were easy to detect in the morning twilight; first as a white flash beneath the dull 'undercast,' and then like gray telephone poles, punching thought the clouds and reaching for the sky," he continued.

Five missiles had appeared simultaneously under Dave's plane, their radar sensors looking for a home.

"Two missiles on the right. Two missiles on the left. One on the nose!" Formation flying left little room to maneuver. The missiles had him boxed in for lunch. Dave had only one option really—put the throttles (all seven remaining engines) to the "firewall" with the hope of outrunning the hungry beasts.

He almost did.

One missile exploded in an orange burst of fire off the right wing. Shrapnel ruptured a fuel cell. Dave killed his No. 8 engine to avoid a fire.

Steve and I were struck with how calmly Dave spoke of his brush with disaster.

I remember this raid and subsequent ones from the radio chatter we monitored on our ship in the Gulf. It was a tense period. Pilots notified each other of missile positions. When a plane was hit, the pilot calmly reported the damage and status. Occasionally, one reported his plane out of commission and begin transmitting on the SAR radio network.

In the first December raids, fifteen of the behemoth B-52 aircraft were shot out of the sky or damaged beyond repair. From December 18th to 30th, twenty-six U.S. aircraft were shot down. Ninety-three pilots and crew were lost.

The emergency airfields in Thailand were already booked up by the time Dave's plane delivered its own lethal cargo. He and his crew refueled the scarred 1959-model B-52 from an Air Force tanker plane over the South China Sea. They nursed the crippled bird all those miles back to Guam. Both tanker and bomber were attacked for much of the return flight because the fueling nozzle on Dave's plane was damaged. For a long period, a fog of spilled jet fuel shrouded the bomber as it refueled.

No planes crashed over the Gulf of Tonkin. We destroyer sailors merely watched the show by radar and listened by radio. After the first three days of bombing, no more B-52s were lost to enemy action. The U.S. Air Force decided by then (with insistence from the pilots flying the missions) that antiquated formation bombing techniques were now passé. Besides, the Communists were virtually out of missiles.

A month later—January 27, 1973—U.S. involvement in the war ended. American POWs in the "Hanoi Hilton," who a month before had cheered as bombs fell on the city around them, were soon released.

In a matter of minutes, Dave and I stepped back in time and went half way around the world to Vietnam to find something in common.

"So, where you from, Dave?"

"A little town in the Florida Panhandle. You probably never heard of it."

"Try me."

"Bagdad."

"Nichol's Seafood, Pond Creek, Blackwater River, Garcon Point, Lapeyrouse Grain Elevator. Naw! Never heard of it! You ever heard of Chumuckla?"

Corporate pilot William David Robertson, Jr., taught at Chumuckla High the fall of 1968. (I missed his instruction by two years.) He graduated from Milton High. My Mother-in-law, Kathryn Gatewood, taught Dave in the third grade. (She tells me he risked life and limb standing on the windowsills at Bagdad Elementary School.)

Even more! His Aunt Kate Haynes Robertson of Milton is my cousin. We're almost related. Small world.

$$\oint\oint\oint\oint\oint\oint\oint$$

THE REAL NAVY

February 1973. My ship, The USS O'Callahan, Destroyer Escort 1051, had completed its Gulf of Tonkin assignments. We steamed across the South China Sea and slipped into Subic Bay, The Philippines.

The harbor was crowded. Our ship's complement of some two hundred sailors could not imagine where all the other ships came from. In our time in this area, we seldom saw any other vessel. Save the few destroyers we operated with for action on the "gunline" or on picket duty, or the occasional mating with a tanker or ammunition supply ship, we assumed the water and the world was our own.

Now, the "Vietnam Thing" was over. The whole Seventh Fleet congregated on the Subic Bay Navy Base. There were Attack Carriers and Helicopter Carriers. We saw Amphibious Assault Ships. There were Refueling Ships, Ammunition Ships and Refrigerator Ships. It was an impressive, gray armada.

All those Carriers in a small port brought a depressing thought. Each carrier contained from two- to five-thousand men. Prices of everything in town would go up two-hundred percent (the simple economics of supply and demand). Already, the sight of the Carriers had our salty blood boiling. "Our Town" (Olongapo City) was under siege by Carrier Sailors.

Maybe it has always been that way. Maybe sailors from small ships have always disliked sailors from large ships. It is certain the "Brown Shoe" officers' corps and the "Black Shoe" officers' corps of the Navy are two different sides of the same coin. The "Brown Shoes" are the Naval Air Corps. The "Black Shoes" are the Surface Navy "Ship Drivers." The "Black Shoe" title is a carryover from the days of coal-burning ships, when the shoes of all fleet sailors, enlisted and officer alike, were persistently black from the coal soot covering the decks. The "Brown Shoe" Air Corps wore clean, bright-brown shoes.

As a rule, Destroyer Sailors do not like Carrier Sailors. I think God planned it that way so they would have something to do if there were no other enemies to do battle with. Carrier Sailors had Bob Hope and all the great USO shows. Destroyer Sailors read about the Bob Hope Christmas Show and other entertainment in month-old newspapers from home. Carrier Sailors never know they are at sea, the ship is so large. Destroyer Sailors wish they could get 50 percent of a submariner's pay because the ship is under water half the time.

You can be sure, however, that in event of enemy attack, a lone destroyer will frantically ask for its "air cover," and a Carrier's captain will anxiously watch for the effectiveness of his destroyer "screen."

And so it was that the crew of The O'Callahan, in February 1973, descended on an establishment called "The Wild East Torpedo Club" in Olongapo City, in the island nation of the Philippines.

The sailors from the carriers were already there, awash in great merriment. There were no Communists. There were no army soldiers. Marines were given "carte blanche" by our crew in nearly every case in those days—probably because of a lingering memory from our last experience in port. From our viewpoint as Destroyer Sailors, there was only one enemy in town, and they were having altogether too much fun!

« »

The humidity was about 97.4 percent. The atmosphere was flared off with a temperature of 91°F. Only an hour out of the showers, the enlisted men's whites were already stained yellow under their armpits. Officers wore color-coordinated brown stains under their khaki shirtsleeves. The air was already ripe outside "The Wild East Torpedo Club," and the destroyer sailors almost congealed the air with odor.

We soon tired of paying double the normal rate for fresh monkey meat on a stick and hundred-year-old eggs. We left the open-air markets and the dusty, crowded, noisy, smelly street in downtown Olongapo City and entered the dank, humid, smelly, noisy, crowded "Club."

Our luck was down and sinking fast. The club was elbow-to-elbow with carrier sailors. We could tell, because they had the name of their ship sewn on their shirtsleeves. They were rowdy. They acted as if they owned the place.

A destroyer sailor, I think a Gunner's Mate, pushed a Boiler Tender from the carrier and respectfully asked him to move aside so he could order a drink from the bar.

"Shove over 'lardhead'—you ain't the only 'something, something, something' in this here 'something something' Navy."

This seemed to create the atmosphere of camaraderie that one would normally expect among Navy men. The "BT" kindly stepped aside, smiled, and motioned the "GM" through the crowd.

The BT said, "I am so sorry I was in your way. Please forgive me. By the way, I see from you shoulder patch you are from the destroyer O'Callahan. Your odor is a profound an-nouncement of your presence. As a matter of fact, your whole ship stinks."

This remark was inappropriate!

The Gunner lost his manners and began to tell the Tender from the USS Constellation (who had 2436 of his buddies in the club with him) that his ship was a disgrace to the Navy and 'something, something, something'".

I had settled at a crowded table, way in the back, from where I observed the refreshment bottle fly across the room. Another sailor broke a chair and began to swing it. The "Country Eastern Band," composed of Filipino starlets, began to pick up the tempo. Some glass broke. The scene was one I'll never forget.

Our Executive Officer, Lt. Cdr. John Heitz, a great leader in combat, announced in strained tones that the junior officers with him might take their drinks and quietly "skulk" out the back door with him. The "MPs" were already pushing in from our flank. He grabbed his drink; I held onto my milk shake. Four of us fled for our lives to the safety of the open streets. A broken bottle of refreshment and three wounded carrier sailors were hurriedly trampled underfoot.

A colorful "Jitney" waited in the alley to taxi a load of inebriated sailors to the docks. We stepped lightly into the super-modified semblance of a WWII Jeep and directed the driver to haul as a demon to the gates of Hades.

We bounced through potholes in the dirt streets, past flashy neon lights, and made several turns heretofore unknown to any of us. The Exec, a mature thirty-four, kept a cool dispo-sition in this time of danger, recognizing the driver's tactic. He was hauling a prize of junior officers, loaded with Ameri-can dollars and fresh new pesos, to a distant alley where his comrades in the Philippine Maffia would relieve us of our trinkets and wallets.

When the Exec explained this, I held my milk shake to the driver's head and crushed it. The driver did not understand the threat. The Exec, who had a more substantial refreshment, broke his bottle over the gear shift and held its sparkling teeth against the driver's neck. He curtly demanded that the driver 'something something something' take us back to our ship or he would 'something something' DIE.

This the driver understood.

Safely returned to our ship, we tried to avoid large crowds for the rest of our brief stay in Subic Bay, in the island nation of The Philippines.

In a matter of weeks after our encounter with the carrier sailors, North Vietnam released the American POWs. Many of them were carrier-based pilots and crew. We were hundreds of miles away by then, in Kaohsiung, Taiwan (a port seldom visited by the big ships). It was then we destroyer sailors felt a great pride in our association with the men of the "Carrier Navy."

§§§§§§§

SOMETIMES IT'S HARD TO BE GREEN

From Pusan to Inchon and Chosin on the Yalu to Wonsan. At least one Marine remembers Korea.

Pat Kilpatrick was a young Marine in 1950. He arrived in Pusan in September of 1950. The United Nations Forces had their backs to the sea. Communist North Koreans had taken all of Korea except for the Southernmost town of Pusan. By

1953, Pat would be an old Marine.

A nervous herd of green-garbed leathernecks, some new to the world of military reality, some hardened on the beaches of World War II, made an orderly move from their ships to take up the enterprise of defense.

Pat remembers a frightened compatriot who decimated an entire platoon of Korean goats in the inky darkness of the first week in action.

Some other observations:

The Inchon Landing, one of the greatest feats in modern warfare, left one Marine with a significant impression of the power of Naval bombardment. "Mighty Mo" (the USS Missouri) fired 16-inch shells that left holes "as big as a house" twenty miles inland.

Somewhere near Taegu, somebody shot a water buffalo. The meat was tough, but very tasty. Months of "C" rations had honed a desire among the troops for "spam on the hoof." The officers never knew about its demise.

General "Chesty" Puller said, "If it takes a "Six-By" (truckload) of dogtags, we're going to take that hill."

"What hill was he talking about, Pat?" I asked.

"I dunno", he said. "Some lil' ol' hill near Taegu."

He doesn't remember the name of the hill, but he does remember that comment made by the general. It did not instill in him a vision of a long and happy life.

Near the east coast of Korea, somebody found a supply of fresh shrimp. Butter was "lifted" from the mess tent. Each marine prepared his own boiled shrimp, cooking it in his own helmet. The shrimp were good, but the combination of butter and shrimp cooked the paint off the insides of the helmets. The paint made everybody sick.

It was cold.

Pat's unit was on the way to the Chosin Reservoir (Frozen Chosin) when the 20,000 troops at the reservoir were overrun by 300,000 Chinese Communists. The shock wave of advancing enemy troops promoted many in positions of power to suggest that the Marines should be abandoned. All available effort should be concentrated on saving troops and materiel near ports of evacuation.

"Chesty" Puller, the Marine General at the scene of destruction—and one of the oldest Marines in service—was told his troops were now surrounded and there was no way out.

"Chesty" said, "That's the best news we've had all day. Now we can shoot in every direction."

Pat was enveloped in what has been called "the greatest fighting withdrawal in all of history." After much bloodshed and a freezing retreat, the survivors (with many thousands of civilian refugees) were evacuated from the ports of Hungnam and Wonsan.

Pat remembers the Korean War. He remembers that in three years, the U.S. lost over 54,000. So far, there is no Korean War Memorial. I wonder why?

§§§§§§§

71

OLD SOLDIERS NEVER DIE...THEY JUST GO FOR ANOTHER HAIRCUT

You want to find some "Old Soldiers?"

Go to your nearest barber shop. Don't go to any establishment that has a name like "Hair-Port 87" or "Guys and Dolls Snip Salon." Look for a place with a name like "Bud's Barber Shop" or "Leon's Barber Shop." No self respecting "Wowotoo" veteran will be seen in one of those "salons." It's gotta say "Barber Shop."

Pop (a "Wowotoo" vet) dragged me into Harold Hudson's Barber Shop in Jay, Florida, on my last trip home. I am pushing 39 years old, and Pop still believes I can't get a decent haircut on my own.

The place was swarming with "Wowotoo" veterans.

I soon established a comfortable slouched position in one of the slippery chairs against the wall. Pop said, "This is my boy, Vic. Vic, that's Ercy Henderson there, and you know Louis Reynolds and Warren Renfroe."

"How Y'all doing?"

I told them I was living in New Jersey now, and I was working for a German company. Ercy told me he had been to Germany once...durin' "Wowotoo."

I can't resist good war stories, so I began asking "dija" questions—like "Whendija?" "Wheredija?" "Whodija?" and "Whadija?"

Private Ercy Henderson said he landed with the 63rd Division at LeHavre, France. (You've heard of D-Day?) The U.S. Army gave him quite a tour of France, Belgium, and Germany. He crossed the Rhine River at Mannheim. The German company I work for (1986) has headquarters at Mannheim. I thanked him for making West Germany what it is today so I could have a job. PFC Ercy Henderson toured Europe all the way to the Alps in Bavaria before the war ended. He noted that the Germans he encountered in his tour of Europe were not as friendly as I have found them to be.

In Italy, Louis Reynolds hauled war supplies with the "Lucky Devils 1924th" transport division. He remembers Anzio, Casino, and Rome. It was not an easy job, driving a truck over a road filled with bomb craters and with the Luftwaffe drilling fifty-caliber holes in the tops of every available target. And Louis was an available target. Tommy, his son, runs an eighteen wheeler now. Sort of a "Chip Off The Old Block."

Pop was in the Navy. He was a crew member aboard a PBY, Submarine Patrol Aircraft with VP84. His squadron flew out of Iceland to cover the North Atlantic Convoys. Pop listened to stories of planes ditching in the North Atlantic and of their crews freezing to death or starving. His goal was to keep every nook and crevice in his plane stuffed with fresh fruit. He didn't stop to think that there would never be time to gather it all if the plane were to crash at sea and sink.

Corporal Warren Renfroe began his tour of France from the bottom of a mess tent garbage pit near Marseilles, where he had jumped to avoid being gunned down. He was coated with odoriferous bacon grease and coffee grounds from head to foot. But after the Messerschmidt strafed his temporary garbage home, there were no holes in his uniform; to him, that was more important. He was with the reconnaissance company of the 629th Tank Destroyer Battalion, attached to the 83rd Infantry. Warren entered Germany from Belgium, passed Aachen, and crossed the Rhine below Cologne. The Rhine crossing was done under strafing and bombing attacks courtesy of the German Luftwaffe. He said he had no problem finding dead people. Corporal Renfroe ended up "The War" about 85 miles West of Berlin.

My heroes are WW-II veterans. They were reared in the economics of post WW-I and grew to maturity in "The Great Depression." Then, the whole world turned into a tinderbox, and the flames of war tempered their metal. They offer the next generation an unprecedented wealth of experience.

$$\oint\oint\oint\oint\oint\oint$$

FROM THE OTHER SIDE

Seated on an airplane, traveling to California on business, I found myself between a black man about my age and a large, gray-haired, ruddy complexioned fellow.

The black man was Lorenzo Howard, a fellow employee from my company. We talked for a long time and discovered that we were both cotton pickers in our youth and that we were both raised not 20 miles from one another. (His story follows later in this book.)

Then I turned to the man on my right.

"You have a slight accent, Sir. Are you a native American?"

"No," he offered, "I was born in Germany."

"Ach!" I exclaimed, "Ich schpreche etwas Deutsch, und Iche Arbeit für eine Grosse Deutsche Firme." [I speak a little German, and I work for a big German Company (1987).]

We struck up a conversation, and soon I simply had to ask..."Sir, you seem old enough...were you in the German Army in World War II?"

Well, he was indeed. He was a Paratrooper, and he was involved in battles following the famous "Battle of The Bulge" as the German Army was pushed back into the "fatherland." The story that evolved was fascinating. Where were Private Ercy Henderson, Sergeant Louis Reynolds, and Corporal Warren Renfroe, of the American Army, now? They would have appreciated this conversation.

In the early 1940s, Gunther Alberts was a "Hitler Youth." He marched in parades, in step with his others his age. They carried brightly polished shovels on their shoulders, just as the German Army soldiers carried rifles.

Gunther was a big fellow. When his age began to show, he volunteered for the Paratroopers. By so doing, he avoided being preselected for the German "SS." Most boys of draft age did not want to be drafted into the notorious "SS."

In 1944 he trained to be Paratrooper. In December of that year, the German High Command launched a major attack against the "American Sector" in Belgium—"The Battle of The Bulge." Early in 1945, Gunther was shipped with his unit by train and truck (the Luftwaffe was, by then, short of airplanes for the paratroopers) to the Belgian border to try to stop the American counterattack.

He described the American Tank tactics for me. He drew diagrams on paper illustrating the effective firepower. The tanks had to stop to aim and fire, but no more than two tanks were still at any moment, as eight tanks pressed the attack.

Gunther watched from his defensive position as his unit was overrun. He watched as a shell blew up the makeshift hospital (farmhouse) he had been in moments before to attend to his wounded comrades. He watched as those who were able ran from the burning building. He watched as the exposed soldiers were cut down by machine gun fire. He watched as the attack moved to envelop his position. Just as his young life appeared doomed, the whole American attack wheeled in another direction and moved away from his machine gun position. He described the battle in great detail, as if the smell of gunpowder were still in the air.

After the attack moved beyond them and left them, in effect, trapped behind American lines, he and his fellow machine gun squad members concluded their war was over. They decided to find some Americans and surrender. Discarding all their armament, they began walking in the direction from which the tanks had come.  Someone had to remind Gunther to drop his "potato mashers"—a supply of grenades strapped to his waist. To try to surrender while carrying any weapon would be a fatal mistake for all of them. They walked several miles to find an infantry unit to surrender to. Some of his first impressions of the Americans:

The Americans had poorly designed helmets that fell off every time the soldiers dropped to the ground. The German Paratrooper's helmet was much better (not like the German Infantry helmet)...it had a snug, round shape, and double chin straps to hold it on the head securely.

The Americans to whom they surrendered were seated and relaxed, 'taking five' in their march to follow up the advance of the armored tanks. There was a blue haze over the entire unit of soldiers. It was cigarette smoke. The sweet smell of Virginia blend tobaccos was new to Gunther, who smoked European cigarettes of Turkish blend tobaccos.

The German Language does not have a soft "R" in it. Somehow, the group of Americans, talking in low tones, seemed to be saying "are, are, are, are, are, are." The soft American "R" was a totally new sound to the young German.

The Americans were eating something all of the time. Constantly, they chewed and chewed. At first, Gunther thought the Americans must always be hungry, and they must have an unlimited supply of food. It was only later that Gunther would discover they were chewing gum.

Because the American's helmets were so poorly designed, the rain would drip off the "pot" right down the collar of the soldier who wore it. Many of the soldiers wore canvas extensions off the back of their helmets to allow the water to drip outside of their clothes. To Gunther, this looked like the uniform worn by "coal stevedores" who delivered heating coal to the homes in Germany.

The story continued with his experience as a German POW, held by the Americans. He told us how he eventually became an American citizen. Leaving the airplane, he asked me, "Did you and Lorenzo really pick cotton as boys?"

I asked back, "Were you really a German Paratrooper?"

$$\oint\oint\oint\oint\oint\oint\oint$$

III

Meet Some of the Folks

"Pity the dispossessed urbanite.
'How's your momma and them?' is an alien question."

Joe Howell married Mary Hanes in 1886. Joe Howell died in 1916, being buried in a pasture. Mary died in 1947. They had four sons and four daughters. Steven died at birth. Duke died and was buried in a pasture. Dessie married twice (first to a Mr. Brock from Pine Log. He died.) Her second marriage was to Jim Campbell. Jim died, but Dessie is still living. Harry Howell was born in 1892 and died in 1971. Ira died and was buried in a pasture along with his brother and father. Prude married a Kilpatrick, Lyda was first married to a Brett. He died and she married again to a Grant. Joe Howell is still living.

*Excerpt from "A History of Chumuckla"
by the Chumuckla Senior Class of 1978*

COUSINS

The events of history span thousands of years. The great books speak of events that changed the world. The minutiae of moments, however, are lost in the evolution of great events. It is the moments, the sum of which equals a single event, which are interesting to me.

For me, specific dates and events do not mesh with absolute correctness in the ether of time. But, the times are punctuated with sharply defined moments. Growing up in northwest Florida meant those moments would involve one or another cousin. Cousins, more often than not, made the moments that led to events.

That is why many of my stories are full of cousins. About forty-eleven of them and a few friends made adolescence an event that could be described as barely survivable.

Our family is blessed with cousins—first cousins, second cousins, third cousins. Cousins once removed, twice removed, and cousins-in-law.

Each year, in my life as an adolescent student, at least one teacher at my school was a cousin—Cousin Margaret Campbell, Cousin Beverly Campbell, Cousin-in-Law Mary Alice Wasden, and more.

There was a plethora of student cousins. Faye and Kittye; David; Clay and Carol; Cynthia and Ronald; Janice, Mahlon, and Gary; and Ronnie—all Campbells. There were Janice and Ronnie Cotton; Vickie, Marty, and Von Griswold; Jennifer, Beverly, Teressa, Floyd, and Neal Enfinger; Jimmie, Nancy,

Lana, Gordon, and Steven Howell. Sammy, Brenda, Mary, and Ann Howell; Martha and Roger Matthews; Cousin Mable Salter; and probably a hundred more.

From this group you will find teachers, nurses, pharmacists, farmers, engineers, scientists, religious leaders, and business people. It is a group of which anyone would feel fortunate to be a part.

If I needed a job, I could work for a cousin. I picked peas, butterbeans, peppers, and tomatoes for one cousin— T. D. Salter. Cousin Campbell Salter and cousin Skeeter Howell hired me to haul hay. Campbell's brother-in-law, Dewey Wasden hired me to pick cotton. When my brother and I planted our own crop of okra, there was no shortage of cousins available for hire.

We helped Cousin Dick Salter with his herd of (not so pastoral) ungulates. When we needed help with our more domesticated, contented cattle, Dick and Tommy Salter and Skeeter Howell's crew were there to lend a hand.

If there is a disadvantage to this sort of "hypercousinivity," it is that you never feel that you can get away with any mischief for long, because everybody knows who you are. The advantage is that you feel as if you belong...and that is a nice feeling—to belong.

Somehow, through several job changes and several cross-country and interstate moves, I have wound up in New Jersey—a state, of course, somewhere north of Georgia and east of Wisconsin. I am told Cousin Vernon Kilpatrick lives in New Jersey.

Even though we live in New Jersey, we have the good feeling of knowing "we belong."

$$\oint\oint\oint\oint\oint\oint\oint$$

MOM'S EXOTIC HOME COOKING

Momma is one of those frus-
trated, creative types who should
have been an artist or a writer.
Instead, she found herself in the
role of homemaker. Her bent
toward creativity can be seen
throughout the house. Pictures
of children and grandchildren
are cut and pasted into large
montages. The furniture is
arranged differently every time I
visit.

And most notably, on every visit home, I am presented
with a new culinary creation. It is a challenge at times to expose my rather bland palate to the innovations my Mom creates in the kitchen. But, I make an effort—to keep Mom
happy, you understand.

I can remember the early days when Mom would fix a new
dish and present it to the family for consumption.

"Ain't gonna eat it Momma...I ain't."

"Come on, just try it," she would say. "You'll like it."

"No thank you ma'am. I just can't eat it. I think I have a
stomach ache."

Usually, we young'uns won, and the children of third
world nations rejoiced as the food was fed to our dog. Dogs
are color blind.

Then Mom found a positive formula for success. She
related the food to one of our latest heroes or interests.

Scalloped potatoes became "Navajo Potatoes," because we recently vacationed among Native Americans in the southwestern United States. Navajo Indians were fresh on our minds. They are a proud band of farmers; and when the need arises, they do not shrink from a fight. The stir fried onions and potatoes became a symbol of their tough spirit.

We had "Howdy Doody Collards," and "Hopalong Cassidy Dried Beans." There was "Mickey Mouse Mush," "Liver a' la Golden Crockett 'Coon Skin," and "Wyatt Earp's Saddlebag Salad."

I have outgrown all that childish pretending though. If I don't want to try one of Mom's creations, I have the maturity, diplomacy, and wisdom, to say..."No thank you, Mom. I'm just not hungry right now." And, I can say it as if I really mean it.

The last time I was home, Mom had gone bananas (and grapes and oatmeal and wheat germ and stuff) with the blender to create a fantastic duplicate of the actual survival recipe carried by Rambo in his search for justice, truth, blood, and the "American Way of Life."

Mom makes the best "Purple Rambo Survival Bug Juice" I have ever tasted.

§§§§§§§

FINDING FATHER

The town of Graceville, Florida, is very close to the Alabama state line. It is a town where the economy depends on the peanut. Years ago the land was known for its timber and cotton production.

From the beginning, how-ever, the town has produced Williamses. The Williams family of Graceville is known all over the United States and in many foreign lands. Their de-scendents can be found almost anywhere, engaged in enterprise or professions that lend honor to their family name.

People who are related to the Williams family are counted among the fortunate. My wife is a descendent of their clan. Her Grandmother, Lucille Williams Gatewood, of Avalon Beach, Florida, was born in Graceville.

Lucille's father, James Henry Williams, was a popular fel-low. He was an educated man. Many believed that his future in Graceville would be a bright one. By the age of thirty, he owned a hardware store in Chipley, Florida—a town not far from Graceville. People called him "BOSS," a nickname he carried from youth.

When Lucille was sixteen months old, her father contracted appendicitis, and in 1907, at the age of 33, he died. For rea-sons believed proper in those days, Lucille was not in atten-dance at the funeral. She was never taken to the grave. Her mother, Georgia Dean, a grieving young widow, was fondly cared for by her dead husband's family. Ownership of the hardware store was lost in a legal maneuver.

After nearly six years, a man by the name of McIvor mar-ried the young Williams widow. He brought her and the child, Lucille, with him to Bagdad, Florida. There, Mr. McIvor worked for the Bagdad Land and Lumber Com-pany as a millwright. Little Lucille soon had a sister, Bessie

Dean, and the two passed their formative years in the mill town of Bagdad, in the balmy climate of northwest Florida.

The distance between Graceville and Bagdad is nearly two hundred miles. In the early part of this century, that kind of distance was not easily traveled, especially across the Florida Panhandle. So, the gulf between Lucille and her father's family grew.

Throughout her life, she and her mother never discussed her father or his death, so painful was the subject for Georgia. A fire burned the McIvor home to the ground. Any records that might have assisted Lucille in learning about her father were turned to ashes. She had never even seen his grave.

After her own children were grown, Lucille began to seek out her roots. She regularly attends the Williams reunion in Graceville (held annually the first Saturday in October). In her visits over the years, however, there was never an opportunity to locate the site where her father was buried. No one could remember, either, in which cemetery he might lie. There were dozens of Williamses in the graveyards. Many graves were unmarked. The possibility that she might never know where her father was buried seemed a reality.

Recently, Lucille received a tip that her father's grave might be in a cemetery in Chipley, Florida. Her daughter, Ann Sanders, and her daughter-in-law, Zanola Gatewood, took Lucille to Chipley on her birthday to help her search once again for her father's grave.

Ann and Zanola started in one part, searching out the grave. Lucille found herself in the older part. There, by a bend in the road, was a large marker. It was her father's. It stated the year of his birth and the year of his death. And below was the inscription, "BOSS." At the foot of the grave, a small marker carried his initials "J.H.W."

Lucille shed tears of joy; her laughter filled the silence of the cemetery. A special peace spread over her. At the age of 81, Lucille feels a sense of completion that had escaped her for a lifetime.

$$\$\$\$\$\$\$\$$

THE MISSING FINGERS

It has been my experience that uncles are a good source of practical knowledge about life. I was always told, by my parents, to listen to my uncles. They would be a good source of information. Lessons could be learned that would come in handy later in life.

And, so it was, I paid a great deal of attention when any of my uncles spoke.

Uncle J. B. Hartzog, who married my mother's sister, Vera Carswell in 1928, proved a prime source of information. He married my Aunt Vera just before the great depression, and he earned a lifetime of experience in only a few short years of absolute deprivation.

They did not know they were deprived. They were so poor before the depression that the stock market crash did little to worsen their lot. They did not have any stock—except an ancient mule that pulled an antique plow in a prehistoric field in Esto, Florida.

Years after the depression, while working in a soft drink bottling plant, Uncle J. B. lost the tip of his right index finger in a bottling machine. The bottle-capping device cleanly severed his finger and bottled it. When Uncle J.B. points out the lessons of life, he points with a short index finger.

Uncle J. B. always said, "Look at the bright side. There is always somebody worse off than yourself. Things are not as bad as they seem."

Uncle Claude Hendrix of Geneva, Alabama, married my Aunt Amie Carswell Howell, whose first husband had died in the '60s. Claude owned the Dixie Dandy Grocery in Geneva.

Uncle Claude is an authority on the town of Geneva. He loves to point out the complex of levees that prevent the town from flooding when the Choctahatchee River and Double Bridge Creek overflow their banks.

Uncle Claude also points out the sights with a short index finger. He lost the tip of his finger long ago, when he picked up a side of bacon while still holding a sharp knife in his hand.

One of Uncle Claude's favorite gems of advice is "It's okay to spend your money, but it is best to spend it on things that last."

Yes, I have learned a great deal from my uncles. Their insights into life and its meaning have been an inspiration to me.

If pressed to say which lesson was the most valuable, I would have to say: "Be very careful where you stick your fingers!"

IN SEARCH OF THE BIGGEST PINE TREE...

Richard Enfinger, a lifelong citizen of Chumuckla, relayed to me one of the most exciting events to happen in those environs in a long, long time.

It seems, according to Richard, that Gordon Howell found himself in a phone argument with Paul Murray at eleven o'clock one night. The argument grew quite loud. Gordon was insistent. Paul would not back down. It was a serious disagreement.

Paul insisted that he had found the largest long-leaf yellow pine tree in Santa Rosa County in the Myrtle Creek Swamp, not far from his home. Gordon insisted he had not, for according to Gordon, the biggest long-leaf yellow pine in Santa Rosa County grew not 100 yards from Campbell Salter's back porch.

"Bet you five dollars."

"You're on."

At a quarter past eleven, the two met at Myrtle Creek Crossing. With two gray, Navy surplus flashlights, they forged into the dark, snake-infested swamp to seek out the Myrtle Creek gargantuan. They trudged through the swamp to a point of high ground, where they found the tree.

"Lordy!" said Gordon. "It is a bigun! But, I think my tree is bigger."

"Well, let's measure it," said Paul.

87

Gordon offered, "We'll have to use *'geomgraphy'*. We'll wait until midnight. With the full moon at its zenith, we'll measure the length of its shadow. With the *'hypothenuse'* of that number times the correction for the mean high tide divided by the square root of its *'circumbulence'*, we will know its height."

Gordon had learned a good measure of mathematics from his brother, Steven, who is a night student at the University.

Paul noted, however, that the moon was only one quarter full that night, and it was cloudy as well. It was best they just measure the distance around the tree. It was big. Gordon was worried. The tree measured 107 inches in circumference at the base.

They left the swamp, following the weak, yellow beams from their flashlights. It was 'dark-thirty' when they reached Campbell Salter's house. They drove their two four-wheel-drive mud-slinging piston-powered chariots as quietly as possible to avoid waking Campbell and Juanita. But they woke up anyway and came out to observe the tense moment of decision.

They shined their flashlights up to the top to try to see its peak. It couldn't be seen. Campbell told them they would have to lie on their backs and look up for two days to see the top of it. They placed the measuring tape around the waist of the tree. It measured 113 inches around. Gordon was relieved. He won the bet.

A few days later, Gordon found a sack of 500 pennies outside his door.

Weeks later, the Salter tree was cut down and sawed into firewood. If only Paul had specified his tree was the biggest <u>living and growing</u> long-leaf yellow pine in Santa Rosa County, he would have won the bet. The mammoth tree had been struck by lightning and was dead. Richard told me the level of excitement in Chumuckla has not been the same for some time now.

$$\oint\oint\oint\oint\oint\oint\oint$$

THEY GAVE THANKS FOR THE RAIN...

You wouldn't think it now. The floods of 1987 have all but erased the memories of the drought of 1986. My Uncle, Duke Lamar Campbell, can tell you about that drought. He'll never forget it.

Last year, for an unbearably long time, there was not a drop of rain in God's Country. My Uncle Duke witnessed the problem first hand. But first, a little about Uncle Duke.

He has lived and farmed in Chumuckla for about thirty-four years of his life. In addition to farming, he ran the local water system for nineteen years. He put in twenty-one years with the Navy. For two years, he was field assessor for the County Tax Assessor's Office; he worked another eighteen years with the county Agricultural Stabilization and Conservation Service (ASCS). In all, he's been working for about ninety-five years.

Uncle Duke saw plenty of water in the Navy...back during "The Big One" (WW-II). He saw more water than he cared to see when he worked for the Water System.

As a farmer in Santa Rosa County, he became accustomed to having water on a regular basis. He and the farmers he associated with talked about water and the weather to the exhaustion of the subject. And then they talked about it some more.

So, it was a disappointment when there was no water in 1986; no rain to talk about.

It was so dry last year the crops begged for a morsel of warm lizard spit from small orphaned lizards. It was so dry, the hay bales came out the size of shredded wheat; condensed hay. It was so dry, Uncle Duke had to add six gallons of water to every bale and stir constantly to reconstitute the hay. It was so dry, in fact, the beef cows in Santa Rosa County nursed their calves on powdered milk.

It was so dry....

The people turned to God for a measure of relief. Every pastor in every church "precipitated" sermons on the blessings of rain. The prayers grew longer and louder. At a church near Berrydale, in the heat of the moment, a preacher forgot himself and failed to cool down his sermon to allow for the already scorching weather. They almost witnessed spontaneous combustion. Almost.

After months of weather devoid of the famous molecules made of two hydrogen atoms and one oxygen atom, a monster storm eased over the Santa Rosa County line. It moved closer. Big stuff! Heavy rain! Aytch Two Oh! Uncle Duke left his work in the barn and took cover in the house with my Aunt Frances.

Timmy Cook, a neighbor, saw it happen. A bolt of lightning burned a brilliant trail through the dark sky, right through the thick fall of rain. It hit the barn precisely on its top and exploded.

Pop saw the smoke next. Uncle Duke and Aunt Frances were soon out in the rain with Timmy and Pop, watching the big barn as it burned to cinders.

Even in the dense rain, it burned like kindling. In a matter of minutes, it was gone. Where once had stood a very large barn, only smoke and steam rose from the ground.

They gave thanks for the rain.

Uncle Duke retires from the ASCS at the end of April...after 95 years of working. I do not think he will rest much though. Aunt Frances says he still has to rebuild that barn.

§§§§§§§

RADIO STARS...

For us, it was a monthly ritual. We would pile into the sky-blue 1955 Ford sedan with Momma and Pop and set out for Bonifay, Florida.

Bonifay is a town that time and Interstate Highway 10 passed by. In my mind's eye, the cooling tower for the ice house is still there. The movie theater is just up the hill from the railroad. There, a kid under the age of twelve could see a movie like "Teenagers From Outer Space" for only twenty-five cents.

It was a two-hour trip. When we arrived, we would visit with Momma's family. We'd visit Granny and eat her special corn bread and sumptuous collards, home grown tomatoes, and butter beans. We would stay with Momma's sister, Aunt Onie B., and her husband Uncle Linton.

Aunt Onie B. and Uncle Linton owned a hardware store in town. They did a healthy business. Most of the profits came not so much from the building materials as from the aged, red and white "art deco" Coke machine strategically placed near the front door. An ice-cold Coke was a nickel, and it was the strongest drink in three counties.

Uncle Linton broadcast a radio show from his office at the store. He was the local radio news anchorman. If anything happened in Holmes County (which was seldom), and if anything did not happen in Holmes County (which was often), the "Holmes County Radio News" would report the details in full.

Just prior to the news was "The 'Slim' Howell Gospel Music Hour," and just after the news was "The 'Slim' Howell Farm Report." Surely, everyone in Holmes County was an avid fan and listener. We kids figured my Uncle 'Slim' Howell had a million fans, maybe even a billion.

That is why we were beside ourselves with pride when Uncle Linton told his radio audience how proud he was of his niece and nephews who were visiting from Santa Rosa County. Aunt Onie B. tuned in the parlor radio for us and we listened as Uncle Linton told the world about his visitors. He told them our ages and how well behaved we were. It was a big deal to hear our names mentioned "on the air."

When we walked into town to see the movie ("The Atomic Man"), we held our heads up high. When people looked at us, the strange kids in town, we knew they smiled because they had heard of us on the radio. They knew we were related to "Slim" Howell—the radio star and news anchorman. We knew that *they* knew that we were "SOMEBODY." It felt good to have a famous uncle.

We returned home to the farm on Sunday afternoon, after one of Aunt Onie B.'s famous Sunday dinners. On Monday, we were back in school. We told our friends about our famous uncle. We told them we were now radio stars because our names were known to millions of his fans and listeners.

Much later, I learned the total population of Holmes County was something under 10,844 people—with 6,743 head of hogs; 4,890 head of cattle; and maybe 43,400 chickens among assorted other of God's creatures. Somehow, that does not lessen the warmth of the memories my Uncle Linton and Aunt Onie B. gave to my brother, sister, and me.

Uncle Linton probably never knew the effect his radio show had on his niece and nephews. But someday soon, I will sit down over a Sunday dinner and tell him how much I appreciate being one of his nephews.

"And Aunt Onie B., could you pass me some more of those collards, please? No thank you ma'am. I don't believe I'd like any more chitterlings just now."

$$\oint\oint\oint\oint\oint\oint\oint$$

DIVINITY CANDY AND PORCH SITTING

Sunday afternoon was sometimes very, very long. It may have been a feature of the decade. Now, in the 1990s, almost every afternoon—and certainly Sunday afternoons—seems to be only a fragment of its former self.

Back in the old days, when Sunday afternoons were interminably long, there were numerous diversions. We could play catch with some cousins or go swimming at Sand Ditch or Myrtle Creek. We might ride horses or sit on the porch with some older friends and relatives. We could sit on the porch at Roy and Idelle Bray's, or Harry and Juanita Howell's, or Roy and "Sissy" Strickland's, or Ruby Robinson's, or any of an infinite number of porches.

There were porches on houses in those days. For those who cannot remember, a porch is a sort of extension of a house that has no walls or windows around it—only a roof. And there was usually a wooden swing on the porch. It was a terribly uncomfortable place to sit and talk, or relax; but there were no air conditioners, or Lazy-Boy re-  cliners, or multimedia home entertainment centers; and people did not know any better. They would sit and visit—and discreetly attack gnats that tried to fly into their ears and noses.

One of my favorite Sunday afternoon pastimes was to ride with Pop over to Cousin Ed and Cousin Ella Enfinger's house. We would pass the schoolhouse and turn left on a dirt road at the cotton gin. Cousins Ed and Ella lived about a mile down the road, across from Uncle Cuyler's place.

The wood frame house, the weathered barn, the leaning corn crib, the azalea bushes, and the aging pecan trees made a picture of the rural South that could represent any old homestead within three hundred miles. But the smell of homemade candy drifting through the house made it a home that could never be identified as anything else but "The Enfinger Place." Too bad you can't photograph an aroma. The aroma of fresh divinity fudge is a memory I need to revive.

Pop must have had a craving for Cousin Ella's Candy. He would sit on the porch and talk for hours with Cousin Ed, while Ella kept us all stocked with fresh divinity candy and coffee. I don't remember what the conversations were about. Maybe politics, or the weather—things that people talk seriously about, but have absolutely no control over.

I don't remember if it rained, if it was cold or warm, who was president then (maybe Eisenhower or Kennedy), or who was county commissioner. The one thing I do remember is that Cousin Ella made the very best divinity fudge I have ever tasted.

It makes one wonder. "What is really important in life, anyway?"

Air conditioning and homemade candy, of course.

$$\oint\oint\oint\oint\oint\oint$$

A RECIPE FOR BLACKBERRY COBBLER

When Aunt Elizabeth (Matthews) refused to go berry picking, I began to understand the importance I placed on the blackberry briar brambles that adorned our fence rows. The fact that my Great Aunt Lyda's sunbonnet had been struck by a rattlesnake on a long-ago berry-picking foray seemed a small excuse to forego the pleasures of a blackberry cobbler. I suggested that she could go bareheaded, thereby sparing concern over her bonnet, but the suggestion had no effect on her decision.

Cousins Roger, Martha, Kittye, and Faye, with Brother Jim and Sister Wanda, joined me in the quest for the very best berries. They were usually in the most inaccessible locations—over a barbed-wire fence or through a mass of briars.

I marvel today at my past ability to walk without any pain whatsoever, through a mass of

thorns and pine cones. I could cross fences easily with a unique two-toed grasp of the wire. My feet had callouses three inches thick. I wore shoes only when required for the sake of appearances—at Sunday School, for example.

As I recall, the recipe for blackberry cobbler was simple.

Pick nine gallons of luscious blackberries that have ripened in the morning dew. Return to Grandma's house with the remaining three berries that were not consumed in the picking process. (Here Grandma takes over.) Place the berries in a big pot and add seven gallons of water and thirty-two pounds of "Dixie Crystal" sugar. Bring the mixture to a boil. Cook until goo.

Grandma made pie crust for the cobbler that was as light as feathers from angel's wings. She combined the goo and crust in a baking dish, creating a crosshatched pattern on top. The concoction was then baked until the smell of the cobbler had driven a ten-year-old to insanity. It was baked ten minutes more for good measure and character development.

The cobbler was dished out with a scoop of homemade vanilla ice cream. The ice cream had to be made in a hand-cranked churn. Electric churns were known to contribute to delinquent children and polarized ice cream.

This is how I remember the recipe. Mom, Aunt Elizabeth, and Aunt Frances (Campbell) have suggested the recipe they use today is only slightly altered from the original.

I have been unable to find a good blackberry patch in the state of New Jersey. I must depend on my memories. But you have the berries. You can pick them. And, now that you have the recipe, you can have a blackberry cobbler. Get out there and pick those berries.

It is only a suggestion, but you might consider not wearing a hat. If you are over thirty, shoes are recommended, but not required.

§§§§§§§

THE GREAT NOMA SHOOTOUT

It was a dreary and rainy week. Aunt Marguerite was a little low. Uncle Cecil's been dead now for over a year, but the memories linger—and they always will. I was thrilled to get her call, to have a chance to chat with the spunky old lady so I could try out my cheer-up skills. I don't know if I cheered her up any, but talking with her for awhile sure made me feel better.

The call reminded me of the story my Uncle Cecil Carswell told me about a year before he died—the story of "The Great Shootout in Noma, Florida." A mild-mannered man with snowy white hair, Uncle Cecil had a gleam in his eye when he told of the pioneer episode.

I listened with awe. This quiet man, with a wry sense of humor, was normally subdued in our crowd of more flamboyant Uncles and Aunts. The others spoke louder than he and overshadowed his presence. But when he spoke of "The Shootout," his quiet voice commanded the room.

Noma was the home of my Momma's family. It was a northwest Florida boomtown—as long as the timber held out. In the 1920s, it was a rugged, noisy, clattering business center that moved money out of trees and into banks. The banks loaned it to farmers who came in to tame the stump-strewn acres of waste.

The Carswells were farmers. They tried, not always with success, to make the earth give up a little more food than the family and the mules could consume. The extra food or fiber would earn money to pay back the banks.

In Noma, as in pioneer towns across the nation, tempers could flare over minor details—like property boundaries. And back then, that's all it took to turn squirrel guns into people guns. A teenage Cecil found himself in a shouting match with a neighbor he did not like anyway. Soon, the war of words led to a showdown. The neighbor went home for a gun; Cecil took the .22-caliber single-action Sears and Roebuck squirrel gun from a wall inside the Carswell home.

The enraged neighbor and the cool, collected Cecil (as he told it), let fly with a hail of bullets, each trying to blow the other to "that bad place." Cecil fired from behind a forked wild mulberry tree in the back yard. The "enemy" fired from a fence until a bullet pierced his hat—a hat for which he had paid good money. While Cecil reloaded, the disagreeable neighbor ran for safety. The next day, he returned with the

Sheriff and pointed to Cecil as a threat to the safety of society and mankind in general. Unknown to the plaintiff, the Sheriff liked Cecil. As the Sheriff peered about the mulberry tree for evidence of empty cartridges, the irate neighbor fumed.

"Can't find any evidence of a shooting, Mister," the Sheriff said as he carefully dug his heels into the sandy soil to bury another shell casing. "I guess you just imagined this young fellow shooting at you."

There was no more argument over the boundary. Noma prospered for a few years and then faded into a quiet crossroads community. Some cattle farms exist, some peanuts are grown. The old town buildings are history. And the story of "The Great Noma Shootout" is a legend among just a few who still remember.

And Aunt Marguerite is feeling a little lonely today.

ϕϕϕϕϕϕϕ

THE OLD RAMBLER DID NOT FLOAT

Cousin Rogene (Pat) Kilpatrick sold me the car in 1969. It was a 1959 Rambler station wagon with push-button automatic transmission. The most impressive thing about the car was its cost—$125. I'm not sure, but I believe Cousin Rogene took a beating on the price. It could be said that this was his contribution to my education.

With the car, I became independent of the 5 a.m. school bus that transported students from the interior of our county to Pensacola Junior College. At last, after nearly two years of college, I had my own car.

The car was a boon to my social life. It was easier to accept invitations from girls in Allentown and Milton who wanted an escort to their church socials. I could repay a girl's gesture later by asking her out to dinner and a movie. Girls were still a bit expensive for my pocket though. Most of my spare cash went to books and tuition.

It was a cheaper thrill to cruise Milton and Pensacola with cousins. Cousins Neal and Floyd Enfinger, Roger Matthews, David Enfinger, Jimmy Howell, other cousins, and friends joined me to cruise northwest Florida, seeking likely places of adventure. We searched for cheap thrills, but never accomplished more than a fraction of our misguided goals.

Things were going well until I sank the car.

Cousin Roger Matthews and I had made plans to camp out near Webb Landing, on the Escambia River. Unknown to us, the river was rising rapidly as a result of the heavy rains that had fallen in South Alabama's Conecuh River basin over the past few days.

As I guided the car into an area known as "Proctor's Wood Yard," near Wallace's Lake, we noticed water crossing the road, but thought little of it. As we moved deeper into the water, Roger suggested that I "reverse engines."

"No, Cuz," said I, "I'm pushing on. We'll find shallow water around the next bend."

As water poured in the doors, I suspected the opposite was the truth, but it was too late.

Soon, Roger and I were sitting on top of the car, watching the water swirl about us. Yesterday's road had quickly become today's river.

I waded out, leaving Roger to protect the car from infestations of alligators and snakes. Soft dirt roads muffled my steps as I plodded for three miles to find help. The only sound was the roar of cicadas, but it was small competition for the churning locomotive (model railroad, H.O. gauge) power of my mind, searching for a believable excuse to explain my situation.

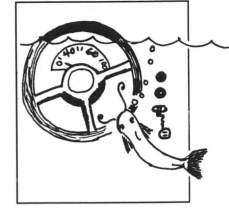

I bore left at Spring Hill Cemetery. Another mile and I crossed Thomas Creek. Up a steep clay hill, around the bend in the road, I passed Cousin Ed and Ella Enfinger's Place. I passed Cousin Donald Campbell's and Uncle Cuyler's. All their houses were quiet. It was past eight o'clock. They would be asleep.

I stopped at Cousin Skeeter Howell's house, where there was a beckoning glow of late-night television.

No excuse would keep Skeeter from laughing as we drove back to my car. His rust and white, four-wheel drive, International Harvester Scout pickup truck was equal to the job. Roger and I were out of the river in short order, with a soaked $125 automobile.

Cousin Roger became an Eagle Scout, but he never went camping with me again.

I knocked $5 off for water damage and sold the car for $120—to Bill Bradwell.

$$\oint\oint\oint\oint\oint\oint\oint$$

REAL TRUCKS HAVE CHARACTER

Pity the poor "pavement pat-sies" with four cylinder (over-head cam), fuel-injected engines, bucket seats, surround-sound stereo, and all-season air conditioning.

Often equipped with four-wheel drive, these toys will never know the thrill of moist earth slung against their under-bellies by worn, mud-grip tires churning to find a modicum of half-dry mud for traction. Nor will they feel a half-inch logging chain nearly jerk the axle out from under their alloyed frame as a knowing and grinning Samaritan, someone like twelve-year-old Wayne Gavin, coaxes his big ol' John Deere tractor to pull it out of an underestimated creek bed.

Jimmy Howell had said, "If you get a running start, Vic, you can reach the other side. No problem." Another time, my brother Jim and I had mired our truck, bumper deep, in a branch of Moore Creek between Pine Level and Bernie Diamond's Store. Mr. Wayne Godwin used his Ford 5000 Selec-tospeed tractor to snatch us from a certain earthly oblivion.

"Skeeter" Howell knows well my attraction to mud. "Like a magnet to a keg of sixteen penny nails," he'll tell you. He pulled me out of Thomas Creek once. He even salvaged one vehicle from the rolling Delaney River for me (previous story).

I remain a proponent of the "running start" theory. But in the confines of Santa Rosa County, and even once in the

Borrego Desert of California (no water at all), the theory has been an embarrassment for me.

Pop's old blue Ford F100, stepside, longbed, pickup truck was a "real truck." Real Trucks come with standard equipment. They tend to bog down a lot. GMCs were more prolific than Fords, especially in Jay; but a Ford was no less the genuine article.

No matter the company logo emblazoned on the hood, you can distinguish a Real Truck from a toy truck through a bit of trained observation. First, and perhaps most obvious, will be "the dent." The dent in the right front fender of our truck was put there by yours truly, a twelve-year old who couldn't judge the distance between posts in a narrow gate. For one thing, I was too short; for another, the hood of the truck was pointed up at a 45-degree angle because of an overload of hay stacked 20 feet high on the back.

My new four-wheel-drive, oriental urban fantasy might never experience an honorable dent. It might be attacked by a BMW as we jockey for position on the Interstate "parking lot." Outside that possibility, my commute from suburbia to a sterile, carpeted, temperature-controlled office in Corporate America will likely be uneventful.

Another obvious clue is patina. The paint on a real truck is not glossy, at least not after a few weeks. Ours developed into an unpolished, almost chalky, remnant of its former appearance. It spoke of "working class" utility. No "candy-colored, asphalt, road toy" that truck! No thirteen coats of high-gloss enamel hand rubbed into its cold-rolled steel.

The corner post holes in our Real Truck were worn rusty raw by the continual insertion and removal of home-built, wooden body extensions. Some dried manure clung resolutely to the inside body of our truck—no matter that our last trip to the Jay Livestock Sale Barn was three weeks past.

An old spare tire rode loosely in the bed of the truck. A shallow pool of rusty rain water lay in its rim. The tire was ready for use at a moment's notice—as a seat for my sister, Wanda, when we made excursions to the swimming hole at Sand Ditch. (I cringe now when I see someone do this. We did not appreciate seat belts then, as we do now.)

The tire itself was a mud-grip retread. Originally, it was a road tire that came with the truck. As soon as it wore down, however, it was taken to the Jay Re-Cap Company on Highway 4 in Jay. There, Mr. Lehman Smith gave it a new lease on life for only $12.98 plus tax.

There was a broken hammer-handle near the tire. Nearby, the hammer head was partially rusted to the bed of the truck. They remained that way for about a year. I guess we figured one day we'd buy a new handle and fix the hammer. The handle came in handy once in the fall. The corn elevator (conveyor) fell on the tail-gate and jammed it shut. We used the hammer handle to pry it open again, proving that broken tools should never be discarded.

A hitch-pin lay next to the tire, half underneath a moldy bale of hay. The hay was still there from our last trip to the "back-forty" to feed cattle. It was the seat of honor, "the first-class section," for the ranking adolescent passenger.

Don't fall for the "gun rack-in-the-window" routine. That, pilgrim, is not a Real Truck. In a Real Truck, the rifle or shotgun will be under the seat in a case, or possibly behind the seat. There will probably be a box of .22-calibre rat shot in the glove compartment. Almost never will a <u>Real Truck</u> have a gun rack in the rear window. That is an illusion created by Hollywood.

A SAFE PROFESSION WITH A GOOD INCOME

In 1959 my cousin, Roger Matthews, first began his foray into the business world. He rented comic books to my brother and me for five cents a copy. They were good ones, too—Superman, Porky Pig, Mickey Mouse, and Donald Duck. He paid ten cents each for them and saved them in a big cardboard box under his bed.

When we came to Milton (The Big City) to visit, we would congregate in his secret profit sanctum, where the cache of comic books was stored. In an hour's time, he could easily make ten cents from me and twenty-five cents from Jim, my brother. Jim was a much faster reader.

Over time, everybody except me grew up. I am as slow a reader as ever and, to this day, have not finished the manual on adulthood (small print; not enough pictures).

Roger decided to study pharmacology in college. He and a number of other cousins and friends suffered their way through Organic Chemistry so they could get a pharmacology degree. I, too, studied Organic Chemistry. But while Roger, Neal Enfinger, David Enfinger, Art Enfinger (lots of Enfingers), and Tommy Weekly were concentrating on what all those carbon atoms were doing with the oxygen, hydrogen, and nitrogen atoms, I was still trying to figure out how to pronounce the name of the sadists who wrote the textbook;. Pharmacology was much too complicated for me.

Now those fellows are all practicing pharmacists in Santa Rosa or Escambia County. I am living in New Jersey, trying to figure out how to pronounce the names of the exits off the Interstate Highway.

One of the reasons Roger went into the profession was because it was "Generally Recognized as Safe." Very few accidents happen to pharmacists. There is little danger on the job—or so one would be led to believe.

In his first five years as a pharmacist, Roger was held up at least three times by drug bandits. They placed a gun to his head and demanded a supply of prescription drugs. As far as I know, those are the only times Roger has every given anything away free.

True to his instinct for business, Roger recently mortgaged himself into ownership of a pharmacy in Milton. I wonder whether there is a comic book rack in the store. Comics today are selling for a dollar apiece.

I plan to inquire whether he will provide a "Lease/Buy-Back" arrangement, or a comic included (plus deposit) with every prescription. Given the current price of a good comic book, that may be the only way I can afford to read them anymore.

$$\oint\oint\oint\oint\oint\oint\oint$$

THE VETERAN COMES HOME

Robert Burgess graduated from Chumuckla High in 1963. His momma owned a little country store. He worked there. The store was in the center of "downtown" Chumuckla, at the crossroads.

It was in 1964 that we began to hear regular news of a place called Vietnam. In a flash, time evaporated. Then, Ol' Robert was in the United States Army. He had a haircut, a helmet, C-rations, shoe polish, dog-tags —the whole 8.2269 meters.

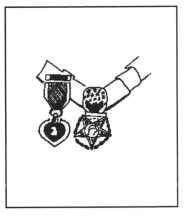

Robert and some other fellows, flush with youthful immortality, found themselves in a live television drama. The world is but a television studio, and we are merely bit-part actors. Theirs was not an enviable part. The show, "Defenders of Democracy in Southeast Asia," aired at 5:30 p.m. Central Standard Time. It was prime-time live, weekdays and weekends, week in and week out.

Robert was trained in portable radio communications. He was sent to Vietnam "posthaste," genuinely attracting our attention. Everybody, especially all the junk food addicts, knew Robert. He was one of us. We had done business with him. We bought "Nehi Grape" belly washers, "Milky Ways," "Tom's" salted peanuts, and "Atomic Fire-Ball" jaw-breakers from Robert.

We started to watch the Nightly News in earnest. Me and Junior, and Paul, and Jim, and Benny, and Tim, and well— most fellows in the pimple population of that locale, began a weekly pilgrimage to the country store. Robert's momma received regular weekly letters from her son. They were postmarked Vietnam. Yes, we took a personal interest in our "man at the front."

Robert was an only son. His momma was widow. Our concern was as much for his momma as it was for Ol' Robert. So, we bought more colas, more cherry bombs, and more candy. We bought anything we could find in the store to spend a nickel on. We felt it was our patriotic duty.

"Bazooka" bubble gum was a particular favorite of mine. I chewed with unabashed vigor as Robert's momma read to us the latest information from the letters. One night, Robert even made a personal appearance on the TV news. An alert citizen of our town spotted him among a bunch of soldiers being interviewed on the glowing screen of a 19-inch black and white television set. A war correspondent stuck a microphone in front of them. The interview gave us conversation material for a month. At last, we concluded, somebody from Santa Rosa County was a television star.

Without explanation, Robert's letters stopped. There were none. Weeks went by. His momma was sick with worry. The television news reported more casualties. The numbers kept adding up. The next letter arrived at last. In it, Robert told how he had accidentally cut himself on his machete in the jungle. The cut, he explained, became infected. He had to spend some time in the hospital. He said he was healing up nicely. In a little while, he would be like new and back at work. We were all happy Ol' Robert had not been shot.

« »

A page turned. A new chapter started with the summer of 1967. School was out. I was now a high school graduate. I started night classes at the junior college. In the daytime, I tended vegetable truck crops with Pop. The money helped pay for school. Pop had an especially good crop of "Sugar Baby" watermelons. The "Clemson Spineless" okra was noteworthy as well.

I remember that humid day as we stacked melons in the back forty. Sweat was rolling out of my short hair and down my back, gluing my shirt to my body. It was hot.

We heard a shout. It came from the neighboring field. Neither of us could see who it was. We walked over to the fence. We waited there for the fellow crossing our neighbor's field. He came toward us. It was Ol' Robert.

He had a broad grin across his sunburned face. Ol' Robert seemed at home in the soggy heat. Not a drop of sweat beaded on his face. He was home from the war and was visiting his family. Ol' Robert's sister, Mary Ellen, and her husband, John A. Cook, owned the farm next to ours.

I asked Ol' Robert a question he would hear again a thousand times. It is a kind of test question. It is perpetually asked of every veteran. The interrogator poses the question innocently. Then, he waits for an answer. If the answer is good enough, the veteran is given a nod of approval, even if the person giving the nod has no personal reference of his own for judging the answer given.

"Did you see any action?"

"Oh, a little," he said.

I nodded. I told him we were all mighty glad he hadn't been shot. Then I asked him how his machete wound was doing. He told us the "machete wound story" was just for his momma. In fact, he said, he had gotten himself shot. Robert asked us to keep that to ourselves. The Sergeant with a "Purple Heart" and a "Bronze Star" did not want his momma to know just yet that he had told her a little white lie.

Pop gave Ol' Robert a watermelon. He told him he hoped he would enjoy it. All of Chumuckla was "beaucoup" proud of Ol' Robert.

109

I grew up with war veterans: Pop, uncles, cousins, and neighbors. But this was the first time I had talked with a recently returned veteran. Ol' Robert was somebody I knew. Looking back, it seemed a subdued homecoming—not at all like movie homecomings. Where was the band? Where was the music? Where were the crowds?

Just a watermelon, and "welcome back."

« »

Pop says it was pretty much that way when he and Wiley Diamond came back from the Second World War. My uncles and my cousins told me about similar experiences from World War I through Korea. Family and friends were happy to see them home again. They voiced some concern and they bestowed modest admiration. They often extended a small token of gratitude. Then, the veteran was expected to start up again where he had left off.

From 1965 through 1974, the people of our county experienced, individually, the quiet ritual of homecoming Vietnam veterans. The entire community, however, showed up for Charlie's return in the summer of 1966. Charlie, Senior Class of 1964, was a star basketball player. He was a gifted fast-ball pitcher on our school baseball team. His homecoming did not bring a joyous gathering of friends.

Charlie Hatfield came home accompanied by an honor guard. Draped over his cold steel coffin was the crisp red, white, and blue flag of the United States of America. For Charlie, an unheralded return, alive, to feel the warmth of a few friends and family, was not to be.

Burgess's Store burned down in the spring of 1971. The crossroads are still there.

§§§§§§§

"DOC" RETIRES...

I once thought about becoming a veterinarian myself. It seemed easy enough. It turns out the medical part is pretty easy, but the human psychology part is mastered by only a few.

An older lady with a pointed nose brings her dog in. "Oh, Doc, she is such a sweet thing. She never bites. Bitsy! Bitsy! Turn loose of the nice doctor's hand!"

Doc Matthews has another typical day. "That will be ten dollars Ma'am; Bitsy just needs half an aspirin twice a day for a week. She is a cute little ol' dog," he says—as he flushes the bite wound with iodine solution.

"That's highway robbery, Doc. Nothing wrong with my Bitsy but eye strain, and you make me buy my own aspirin and charge me $10. You ought to be ashamed, you mean old man. And Bitsy was so calm before we came to see YOU! Now look at her, she's a nervous wreck."

"Next, please," says Doc from the office door.

Two human "pups" about seven and eight years old spill from the back of a beat-up station wagon lugging a graying cocker spaniel in a box between them. The dog has been hit by a car. Leg broken; gash on face; some teeth knocked out. The kids are in tears.

111

The mother of the two children looks distraught and stunned. Out of hearing range, she tells Doc to do what he feels is best; if he must, just put Ol' Rosey to sleep.

Doc looks at the children. He looks at the dog and back again.

Two hours later, the dog is full of stitches, iodine solution, and antibiotics. The leg is set. Ol' Rosey is carefully carted back to the car and will survive a few more years of family love.

"Ten dollars, Ma'am".

The phone rings.

"Doctor Matthews, please?"

"Speaking."

"My sow is heaving and panting and laying on her side. We just moved here, and this is our first farm. Can you come help us, right away. I think the sow is dying."

"Have you ever witnessed a birth?" asks Doc.

"Uh,...no."

"Get you some dry rags if you want, and dry the baby pigs off as they are born," advises the doctor. "Let me know how you make out."

Dogs that bite, cats that scratch, pigs that stink, and cows that wear you out. And, sometimes, people who appreciate.

My Uncle Olyn ("Doc") Matthews retired from the practice of veterinary medicine. I suppose, now that he has *practiced* for so long, he will attempt the real thing.

§§§§§§§

THE FESTIVAL OF "TWO-TOED TOM"

People are apt to celebrate just about anything under the sun. In the town of Esto, Florida, on the first Saturday of September not long ago, the people of that area celebrated the memory of a legendary monster alligator called "Two-Toed Tom."

Nobody, that is nobody alive, can recall ever having seen the gator. Only his tracks were left—evidence of his wanderings, his thrill for excitement, and his appetite. Why, it is said that in 1919 no decent pig or chicken could feel safe within 200 yards of any body of water in Holmes County. According to legend, one of the gargantuan  gator's feet left a print with only two toes. Why only two toes? Maybe he lost the other three in a deadly encounter with a Micropterus salmoides (Largemouth Bass) when he was but a hatchling. Who knows? But, the track with two toes gave him his name.

My momma's brother, E. W. ("Tobe") Carswell, a gifted historian and well-known writer in Florida, lives in retirement in Chipley, Florida. My Uncle is the one who told me about Two-Toed Tom and how he came to be. In some ways, my Uncle Tobe has been instrumental in promoting The "Two-Toed Tom" Festival.

Uncle Tobe says the gator first showed up in the Esto area in 1916, following what the <u>Chipley Banner</u> referred to as "the most disastrous flood ever to visit this section." It was forever thereafter referred to as the "The July Flood of 1916" or just "The July Flood." Santa Rosa newspaper accounts will verify the extent of rainfall that July. A few miles east of Santa Rosa County, the rainfall was recorded to be thirty-six inches in three days. Some accounts of the period say it was the highest water since the "The Lincoln Flood of 1865."

In Esto a new lake called "Sand Hammock" was formed by the flood. Soon afterward, the unpopular gator was chased from his Alabama home by an angry posse. For a time, the saurian "Tom" made his home in that lake. Uncle Tobe says the alligator fell in love (or possibly hate) with the voice of a sawmill whistle in nearby Noma. Frogs were plentiful following the downpour. The frogs and drowned livestock probably made a full menu for ol' Two-Toed Tom.

Once the free meals diminished and Two-Toe began searching for a more lively diet, his welcome wore out. He carried his two toes—and his haunting bull gator love call—to other parts. He may have headed west, toward Black Water River. In any case, by the time the sawmill whistles were only a memory, so was Two-Toed Tom.

Uncle Tobe says published accounts of the famous gator have been revived for the festival. The people who remember the sawmill era, and those who want to experience the ambience of another time, should take the short trip to Esto in September. Thousands came last year to celebrate the history of the period and the legend of the alligator.

This time there will be an extra performance. The groaning sounds of a bull gator and the Noma mill whistle will be played over a loudspeaker—sounds that deserve to be continued in perpetual memory.

$$\oint\oint\oint\oint\oint\oint\oint$$

CAMPBELL REUNION...

There is usually a "Campbell Family" reunion after church on Labor Day weekend. It is held at the Chumuckla School. Family and friends have an open invitation and are encouraged to bring food (pot luck).

I attended a recent reunion. Saw a lot of my long lost cousins and met a lot of them I didn't even know existed. The food was unbelievably good, although I did not have an opportunity to enjoy it as much as I wanted because I was enjoying the conversations too much. This may explain why Campbells have a tendency to talk with their mouths full. They cannot get enough of either talking or eating.

When there is a reunion in Santa Rosa County, it is almost a matter of etiquette to invite everybody. The reason is, almost everybody is related. If they are not, they are a friend of somebody who is. At the last reunion, there were attendees with names like Enfinger, Howell, Matthews, Norris, Salter, Griswold, Nelson, Coleman,

Cotton, Kilpatrick, Gillman, Howard, Gregory, Driskell, Simmons, Engert, Frazier, Spicer, Jernigan, and Miller—and, oh yes, Campbell.

Cousin Faye Campbell Westfall has lived in Gainesville, Georgia, for many years. She had good intentions of visiting everyone and rekindling relationships. She told me to stay close, so I could tell her who everybody was. I told my brother Jim to stay close to me to tell _me_ who everybody was. He told Pop to stay close.

The plan fell apart when Pop started to chow down on the food and Jim was drawn into a conversation about accounting. Jim's talk of accounting quickly vacated the space around him.

Cynthia Campbell caught Faye off guard and began a conversation. Faye had not seen her in twenty years and had no idea who she was. "And which cousin are you?" asked Faye, with a puzzled look.

"Well, I am your school chum, neighbor, and life-long cousin, Cynthia Campbell," replied an embarrassed Cynthia. An equally embarrassed Faye retired to a chair in a dark corner to eat butterbeans, fried chicken, and cornbread until someone she recognized (like her Mom) came to take her home.

I did not fare much better. I saw Cousin Beverly Campbell and blurted out, "Why hello, Gladys. It is so good to see you!" I don't know why my brain decided to call her "Gladys." Cousin Beverly told me to try again. I got it right the second time.

Calling people wrong names at a reunion, especially when they are among your favorite people, is cause for red-faced embarrassment. My face was crimson. I retreated to a distant corner of the room and reviewed my reunion tactics.

- RULE ONE: Never, never call anybody by name. Force them to spill it in the conversation, or wait for *someone else* to use it. Then it is safe, unless the person you choose to mimic is an imbecile like yourself. I knew better.

- RULE TWO: Never ask them what their name is. Faye should have known better.

- RULE THREE: Even if you believe they should know you better than their own child, introduce yourself and give them something to relate to.

I returned to the reunion determined to live by the rules.

"Hello, so good to see you. I'm Vic Campbell. You know, J. Lee's boy—Lamar's nephew. My brother is Jim Campbell. I have a sister Wanda who married a Yankee by the name of Roberts."

"Jim Campbell? Doesn't he come from Berrydale?"

"No. No. That's Buddy and Lillie's boy, Eddie. He's my cousin—married to Sylvia. They have two daughters named Kelly and Tonya."

"Oh! Then you're one of the Chumuckla Campbells. You live near Copeland Griswold (another cousin), don't you?"

"No, Mom, I'm your son. I live in New Jersey now with my wife, Karen. She's a Gatewood from Avalon Beach, who is related to the Tinsleys, the Burnetts, and the Joneses."

"Oh! _That_ Vic Campbell. The one who visits home so seldom."

§§§§§§§

SKEETERSONIAN MUSEUM OF CHUMUCKLA

You do not have to travel to Washington D.C. to visit the Smithsonian Museum or the National Archives to get a taste of American History—only to Chumuckla—the nerve center of Santa Rosa County, Florida—and have a visit with Skeeter Howell.

Skeeter has an impressive collection of Americana—of a sort that can be found in no other collection in the world.

I have seen documentaries on television of the SS Andrea Doria, a luxury liner that sank in the Atlantic in 1956. People have stared bug eyed at their television sets to view fuzzy submerged camera views of the ship. Skeeter has an original life vest from the doomed vessel in his collection. His cousin, Floyd Enfinger, was a crew member of a navy destroyer that picked up survivors. He saved some life vests after saving some of the passengers.

Most of us are familiar with the tragedy of the "Hindenberg," the great dirigible that burst into flame over Lakehurst, New Jersey, in 1937. Thirty-five people were killed. A photograph of the incident remains one of the most vivid documentations of human tragedy.

One of Skeeter's friends, Carl Nesbitt, was a teenager, handling control lines on the ground as the "Hindenberg" made its attempt to dock. After the explosion and the confusion, he found the charred remains of the compass used to guide the "lighter-than-air" craft. Now, the compass is in Skeeter's museum.

As you tour the museum, Skeeter will point out things that might otherwise escape you. There's a "Sheepskin" land title, issued in 1902 and signed by Theodore Roosevelt. You'll see a 1920s model hay bailer that used wire to bale the hay.

In his menagerie, he has a spinning wheel used by my Great Grandmother Howell. Uncle Joe Howell donated several crosscut saws that were used in the county early in this century. "T. J." O'Kelley gave the museum several items he found at the remains of the old Wolfe Creek Stage Coach

Stop. Ask, and Skeeter will tell you something about the old stage coach route.

Mr. Henry Gilmore of Mulat visited once and was most intrigued with a 1925-vintage photograph of the Pensacola Fire Department. He recognized some of the people in the picture, having worked with them as a fireman in the 1930s.

Mr. Willie Bell (who died some years ago) found a Civil War Enfield rifle in a hollow tree near his home in Pattersontown. (Long before the present, skirmishes between people who disagreed took place in this area.) The rifle had actually "grown" into the tree. Rifle and shot sack were carefully recovered. The shot sack disintegrated; but rifle and shot are now on display in the Skeetersonian—a gift from Mr. Bell.

Skeeter is in the phone book, under Laverne Howell. He enjoys talking about the history of the area. But then, he enjoys talking about most anything. If you enjoy listening, a visit to the Skeetersonian can make a perfect combination.

Visiting dignitaries, properly announced, may experience the added pleasure of a cup of coffee from Skeeter's wife, Laurel.

IV

Someplace Else

"From Chumuckla Crossroads, you can go anywhere in the world. You can go up to Atlanta. You can go to Detroit, San Francisco, New York, or Paris, or China—or even to Alabama. If you don't like it here, you can leave."

As told to Mac Ryals
by his grandfather, J. D. Ryals

"You can't get there from here. You have to go to Atlanta first and then take a sharp left turn."

THE STATE UMPIRE BUILDING

Recently, our nephew Christopher Gatewood, age 8, flew in an airplane for the first time. He and his Grandma Gatewood came to New Jersey to visit his Aunt Karen and me.

Aunt Karen took Chris and Grandma to see the Amish farm country in Pennsylvania. Then they visited Philadelphia to see the Liberty Bell and Independence Hall. They boarded Admiral Dewey's old battleship, the USS Olympia—a relic of the war with Spain.

I took them all to Long Island one day. We crossed Manhattan Island with its many canyons created by a maze of tall buildings. We went to a place called Oyster Bay. The historic home of the twenty-sixth President of the United States, Teddy Roosevelt, sits on Sagamore Hill, overlooking the bay. After touring the museum there, we came back to Manhattan and visited the Natural History Museum.

Christopher, being an intelligent fellow, was quite observant and absorbed all the information we could give him. Karen and I, not yet having children of our own, enjoy these brief visits from our nephew and nieces. It is one of the few opportunities we have to impose our own view of history and the way the world works on the younger generations.

However, our educational efforts are not always interpreted as precisely as we present the facts.

Christopher told me of his visit to Philadelphia. He said, "Uncle Vic, I have seen the *Independent* Mall and the *Livery*

121

Bell. And I went on this big ship. I want to be a *General* in the Navy when I grow up. Did you know they have *"chollies"* (trollies) in Philadelphia and you can ride them all over the city?"

Well, at least the kid got one thing right. If you're going to join the armed services, the Navy is the way to go. I was not satisfied, however, with his education under the tutelage of Aunt Karen and Grandma. I took it upon myself to explain our tour of the Roosevelt museum and provide an historical narrative for the boy.

Later in the day, he expressed his appreciation for the tour of *Teddy Ruxpin's* home at *Sycamore* Hill. He said the view of the Statue of *Livery from the Lincoln Funnel* left something to be desired. But, the National *Geographic* Building was great, and after he had seen the *State Umpire* Building— the tallest building (in *New Jersey?*)—he was satisfied this was one of the best days of his life. He could hardly wait to return to Pea Ridge and tell his brother Jason, age 6, all about the trip. He wanted to tell him all about this big country, the United States of America.

Maybe Christopher's view of history isn't so bad after all. Frankly, I enjoyed it.

As I always do after any of my nieces or nephews visit, I extended to him a hearty invitation to come again—as soon as he finishes college.

MOMMA CAME TO THE CITY

Living in New Jersey can be exciting. It is only a short trip to New York City, where the excitement is as thick as the peanut butter that sticks to the roof of your mouth.

Awhile back, Momma came to visit us in New Jersey. I wanted to show her how nice the place can be. Her first impressions, however, were obstacles to her acceptance of the pleasantries that abound here.

Perhaps I should have driven my car to the airport. But at the time, I was not acclimated to the maniacal stress of these New Jersey roadways. I chose to take a train into Newark and then a connecting van over to the airport, where I would meet Mom. Together we followed the same route home.

Mom looked dazed as she came from the airport terminal. Downtown Chumuckla was already over a thousand miles away.

We hugged. I took the bags from the luggage carousel as it coughed them up. We made our way to the metro connecting van pickup point. After waiting forty-five minutes, we boarded the van that would take us to downtown Newark and the train connection. It was already near midnight.

As the van passed down Broad Street, I tried to explain to Mom that not all of New Jersey was like this, a puzzle of old buildings, rough streets, and urban decay. We have trees near our house, I explained.

The van stopped for a traffic light. The van driver, a woman, called our attention to a lady of the evening standing on the corner opposite us, beside a large church. She was exposing herself (rather completely) to the driver of a tractor trailer who was also stopped for the traffic light.

Momma pressed her hands and face against the windows of the van to get a better view. She was a real "you know what" and this was not a TV show; it was real life. The truck driver loosed a bellowing blast from his air horn. Momma had never seen anything like it. The van driver, a native of Newark, expressed disbelief as well. Seems such extreme exposure is a rarity—even in Newark.

"Well," I said, "I don't think she's over there to teach Sunday School."

We soon left the van. In the darkness of the Broad Street Train Station, in a rough section of the city, we waited for the train. "No Ma, I ain't scared...scared...scared," I whispered, with a hollow echo repeating quietly from the dark city walls beyond the station. It was a nervous wait before the train arrived to take us from the metropolitan area into the hills, where we could "de-tense" our nerves. Forty miles out of the city, we left the train. I brought Momma the rest of the way home by car.

These days I drive my car to the airport to pick up visiting friends and family. But the fear of being mugged in the metro area has been mitigated somewhat. Since the stock market crash of 1987, many of the muggers are ex-brokers, inside stock traders, and yuppies down on their luck. It is somehow comforting to know that today's upscale muggers are dressed better than I am, more often than not. It takes some of the edge off the fear factor.

Momma did see better sights as her visit continued, although her mental picture of the area still carries the flavor of Broad Street in Downtown Newark at midnight.

§§§§§§

THE WILD SIDE OF NEW JERSEY

My brother Jim and his family were here in New Jersey a few weeks ago. They did not want to see New York City this time. Jim said the wildlife there was too much for the boys, Ben (age 9) and Kevin (age 6).

Jim and the boys enjoy museums, especially natural history museums. Jim's wife, Lynne, has seen more museums than any other living human. Mention the word and Lynne's left eye begins to twitch.

I told Lynne we were going into the country to see some museums and look for rocks (her right eye twitches at the mention of rocks). Lynne decided to let us go on our own, unsupervised.

We stopped somewhere deep in the Delaware River Basin to examine a pile of rocks. The boys found 7823 rocks and a dead meadowlark suitable for their collection back home. After sorting through the rocks, Jim narrowed the choices down to thirteen. We had to leave the twenty-five ton boulder and the dead meadowlark, but only under protest.

This part of New Jersey is surprisingly rural and unspoiled. Driving through the forest, we spotted nine deer. Only one of them had been run over by a car.

At one point, we found a five-foot-long black snake crossing the road. I stopped the truck, ran to the snake, and grabbed it by the body. I slung it about just a bit to keep it from biting me. The snake then calmed down and gave the boys a lesson on what a nonpoisonous snake looks like.

Out of every hundred snakes you see, ninety-nine are of a harmless variety that helps to maintain a balance of nature. They are really quite helpful. Of course, the few snakes that are poisonous should be avoided. But they, too, contribute to the balance of nature. The poisonous snakes are dangerous to people, but more often than not, people are more dangerous to the snake.

We didn't take the snake with us. We turned it loose in the field beside the road. Besides, when the word "snake" is mentioned around the boys' mother, her neck begins to twitch. We continued our tour of the wilderness. We hiked a trail to look at waterfalls. We visited a "rock shop" and bought some fish fossils and Indian arrowheads. After a brief pause to pump more air into the tires on my truck, we loaded our additional haul into the back. We did not manage our time well enough to visit a museum that day.

When last seen, Jim, Benjamin, and Kevin were grinning with menace as they headed for Washington, D.C. There, they would visit the Smithsonian Museum, which has a marvelous display of rocks and snakes. The "mummy" tied in the right front passenger seat had, by then, developed an obvious, spasmodic, body twitch.

§§§§§§§

IS THERE A SANTA ROSA COUNTY?

I find the people we call "Yankees" to be an interesting lot. Most believe the world begins and ends between New York City and Boston. The center of the universe, according to adherents of the "Manhattan Sect," is the corner of Fifth Avenue and East 50th Street in New York City.

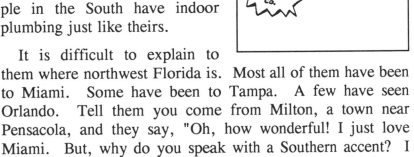

Yankees are generally slow in all that they do. For instance, up North, it can take at least six months to buy and close on a house. It can take two years to remodel a bathroom. But they are proud of their bathrooms. They express disbelief that people in the South have indoor plumbing just like theirs.

It is difficult to explain to them where northwest Florida is. Most all of them have been to Miami. Some have been to Tampa. A few have seen Orlando. Tell them you come from Milton, a town near Pensacola, and they say, "Oh, how wonderful! I just love Miami. But, why do you speak with a Southern accent? I never heard a Southern accent in Florida."

I have begun to tell them I am from L.A. ("Lower Alabama"). The mental picture they have of Alabama is closer to the Santa Rosa County I know—cotton, peanuts, soybeans. Yankees have a very limited knowledge of geography. I often resort to drawing a verbal map of the United States to explain where northwest Florida is.

"You know where California is?" I question.

"Yes," they say, indicating some knowledge of geography.

127

"New Mexico?" "Yes."

"Arizona?" "Yes," they say as they begin to tire of the mental exercise.

"Well, the next state over is Texas, and The West Florida Panhandle is stuck right up against Texas except for little chunks of Louisiana, Mississippi and Alabama that get in the way."

"Oh!" they exclaim with the delight of a new discovery. "So Tampa is right next to Texas, almost. Well, I'll be mugged in Central Park."

I have accepted the shortcomings of the Yankees. We can't all be as cultured as the people of Santa Rosa County, Florida. We know where Pensacola is. And if anybody asks, we can even give directions to Brewton, Alabama.

And we know what it's like up North, too. Besides me, Bubba's been here. He'll tell you the entire state of New York is covered with concrete and skyscrapers. He'll say once you've seen Boston, you've seen all of Massachusetts.

Yankees will tell you that New York State has some of the largest expanses of wild forest you'll see in the United States, some of the wildest rivers, and some of the best farmland. According to Bubba, they'll tell you similar lies about Massachusetts and New Jersey.

I'd be careful listening to those kinds of people. You know—Yankees. They have no idea that the center of the Universe is, in fact, somewhere within a twenty-mile radius of the Chumuckla Crossroads.

§§§§§§§

THE YANKEES RESPOND

After my column on Yankees appeared in The Santa Rosa Press Gazette, the paper was deluged (sprinkled?) with comments. A sampling of the words of supporters and detractors follows.

Annoyed With Campbell

"...I was quite annoyed, but as I read on I realized that whoever this Vic Campbell was, he had to be, first of all very narrow minded and lacking gravely in the CULTURE and class department."

She strongly suggested that I buy a Webster's Dictionary and noted that Mr. Webster was a "Yankee.

"Mr. Campbell, you really don't know what you're talking about when you criticize the people and places you mentioned in your article. I feel sorry for someone like you who can't see the forest for the trees.

"Fortunately, Mr. Campbell, the majority of Americans are NOT narrowminded like you and that is why we live in the greatest nation on earth.

"By the way, 'Yankee' is (Webster's Dictionary) and one of the meanings is 'a native or inhabitant of the U.S.'. And rightly so; any American who served overseas in World War II will tell you they were referred to as 'Yankee' or 'Yank' even if they were from Chumuckla." *Donna Dagnell, Milton, Florida.*

« »

Really Annoyed With Campbell

"We direct this to Vic Campbell and believe his verbal map of the United States ends in Brewton, Alabama."

They went on to say there is a "Milton" in Vermont and an "Ipswich" in Massachusetts (a historical town which was once their home).

"How blessed these 'Yankees' have been that our children grew up skiing at Stowe in Vermont and never had to worry that Santa would come any other way but by sleigh for every White Christmas.

"Seventeen years ago we chose Northwest Florida as our place in America. We feel we have the best of two worlds. Our grandchildren have all that the North offers, plus our beautiful Gulf Coast. They can visit Mr. Golden's Cotton Plantation and can take little bales of cotton back to school. It's nice to share with them a little part of your world, Mr. Campbell." *The Tremblays, Milton, Florida*

« »

Writes To Support Campbell

"When these people came to our beautiful community to escape from rottencold Massachusetts, they should have been prepared to accept a little good-natured kidding. I've lived here for six good years and have found wonderful neighbors and friends. A little joshing now and then hasn't been too great a price to pay.

"Don't let a couple of sour apples discourage you, Vic. Keep those fine articles coming." *Al Homan, A Reformed Yankee.*

« »

I, Personally, Like Vic's Columns

"Dear Annoyed: I...understand your reaction....No matter how light-hearted the column was, it still touched a nerve.

"I am sure that the column was not written with the intent to degrade the good people of the north. I have heard from time to time, myself, ribs and prods (from northerners) about being a dumb southerner from a hick town (that I happened to be proud of) and no one had never heard of. I learned to laugh at these comments because most were light-hearted humor. No harm intended.

"So don't make a mountain out of a mole hill. We ARE all Americans and our humor or our ability to laugh as well as cry together is among our greatest attributes.

"I...like Victor's columns and enjoy his...type of humor. A wise man named Lin Yutang once said 'There is purifying power in laughter—both for individuals and for nations. If they have a sense of humor, they have the key to good sense, to simple thinking, to a peaceable temper and to a cultured outlook on the world'." *Roy G. Griswold.*

෫෫෫෫෫෫෫

A CULTURAL EXPERIENCE

Bubba has informed me of a vitriolic response from some of the readership regarding my recent column about slow Yankees. I must apologize, for there were some errors in the column. The tempers of some of my observant fans were, understandably, overheated by my aggravating remarks.

As yet, I have not received the issue of the paper with the column in question, nor the one in which the responses were registered. The comments following are based completely on hearsay.

One reader pointed out that I should immediately purchase a "*Wilbur's* Dictionary." She inferred it would clear up my misuse of the word "Yankee." I believe she was quoting from the unabridged, international version, when she noted the word "Yankee" referred to all people of United States citizenship.

I rushed to the local bookstore to buy one. The unabridged, international version was not available, but I did locate an abridged, pocket-size, regional version for seventy-five cents.

While standing in line, I looked up the word "Yankee." As I recall, it clearly stated that "Yankees are a large body of people who are native to the northern environs of the United States of America. When enlightened, many choose to move to hospitable areas such as northwest Florida, where they live happily ever after."

After waiting in line for an hour (I live in New Jersey, you know) while the clerk filled out a charge form for the customer ahead of me, I gave up on the book and laid it aside.

In place of the dictionary, I purchased a 1988 "Plastic Homeowner's Magazine" semiannual swimsuit calendar. It was on display at the counter. The cost was reasonable, only $17.95 plus all applicable State and local taxes (total bill $37.82). I felt the calendar would get more use than a dictionary.

One reader hinted that I was not an educated person. It took three summers, but I did graduate from "The New Bethel Baptist Church Vacation Bible School." They called it a "social promotion," but my diploma will stand up against any other Vacation Bible School in the whole country—and some parts of California.

I graduated "caveat emptor" from Pensacola Junior College, "nolo contendere" from the University of West Florida, and "persona non grata" from The University of Florida. Surely, Harvard could provide no better education.

I have nothing against Yankees. I have a number of frien... er...acquaintances who are Yankees. In addition, my sister-in-law and my brother-in-law are Yankees. They are surprisingly nice people, for Yankees.

Perhaps I was in a fit of rage when I wrote the column on slow Yankees. Living in the most misunderstood state in the union (New Jersey) can be trying for a Southern fellow. I never had to wait in line for an hour in the South—not for a book. In the South I have often waited in line for a swimsuit calendar—but never for a book.

It is obvious to me that the Yankees who wrote in response to my column are not at all slow or lacking in culture. I would be pleased to call them frien—er...acquaintances.

My wife burned the swimsuit calendar.

§§§§§§§

SANTA ROSA HAS THE BEST OYSTERS

Well, I remember shoveling oysters from shell to salty cracker, heaped with a healthy dose of horseradish and catsup, and I remember chugging the lovely morsel down the hatch with a fizzing cola chaser. Ah! Those were the days.

133

Often in the late 1960s, after I had studied Invertebrate Zoology at "The Junior College" under Professor Keitz Haburay, I would investigate the fibrillating heartbeat of the little animals as they lay in their shell, waiting to slip into oblivion. If the oysters were not eaten at this point, they would have *died*.

It was at an oyster fest with Curt and Letha Myers and my folks that Pop encourage me to describe the parts of the oyster to Curt. A small sea worm of the genus Neris slithered across the oyster as I spoke. I pointed out the worm and gave a little discourse on the nature of its many legs.

Maybe it was because of the great interest in my new-found knowledge of sea creatures, or maybe it was because of the low light, but few oysters were eaten that night. Ate a lot of crackers though! Curt used to really like oysters.

No more do I lecture on the little buggers. I just eat 'em. I think my fellow oyster lovers appreciate the silence as we gorge ourselves on these morsels that team with natural alpha tocopherol. (Vitamin E is suggested as a cure for a lot of things, including skin problems, but I do not recommend rubbing oysters all over your body.)

An experienced oyster eater can name the very bay from which his pelecypod was harvested. A given species of oyster, and there are many species, will carry a different flavor, depending on the river that feeds its estuarine habitat.

Pliny the Younger, the great Roman Orator and nephew of Pliny the Elder, wrote about Sergius Orata around 100 A.D. Sergius is one of the first people in recorded history to have cultivated oysters.

The Romans were quick to spot a good meal. Take spaghetti, for instance. Marco Polo walked halfway around the world to borrow the recipe from the Chinese. I question, however, the Italian love for calamari (squid). Decimus Junius Juvenalis, a Roman poet, wrote a little ditty about an epicure of this time:

> *He could tell*
> *at the first mouthful*
> *if his oysters fed on the Rutupian*
> *or the Lucrine bed*
> *or at Circeii.*

I'll vouch for it. There is a restaurant under Grand Central Station in New York City called, appropriately, "The Oyster Bar." There, you can sample oysters from all over North America. I recently had a small serving of Apalachicola oysters there. They cost seventy-five cents each though, so I did not get my fill. Apalachicola oysters are a less filling variety. But they are a world class above the taste of a Chesapeake or Blue Point oyster.

Santa Rosa Countians are lucky. The very best oysters of all come from East Bay. Fed by the pure stream of Blackwater River, and flavored with the saline spice of the Gulf of Mexico, they have no equal. And, they can be had for less than three dollars a dozen—on the half shell.

Decimus, Junius, Juvenalis, and the Pliny Boys would be proud.

ϕϕϕϕϕϕϕ

135

YANKEE EXPERIENCE

I take some ribbing occasionally from the Yankees at work. So it is only natural that I would want to "fire a broadside" back once in awhile. One time I wanted to go up to a Yankee and tell him just what I thought of Yankees. (Why is it that when I get in the mood, all Yankees appear to be eight feet tall?)

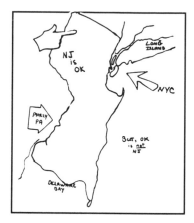

I fortified myself with some "Rambo Oat Puffies" and thrashed out my feelings on the typewriter. Normally, such outbursts of thought wind up in my trash can. This time, however, they wound up in print, in front of God and everybody in Santa Rosa County.

I wasn't thinking (my wife says that's normal). Only intelligent Yankees would live in Santa Rosa County, which to the best of my knowledge is "The Center of The Universe."

The People's Republic of New Jersey has a plethora of very nice folks—and some of the prettiest landscape in the country. I don't know where *Dipswitch, New York*, is (which one reader mentioned in reply to my column), but I can show you Waterloo, New Jersey. I'll bet Waterloo is a fair match.

I can stow a canoe on my truck and, within forty-five minutes be on a secluded lake atop the Appalachian mountains, fishing for bass or pike. I can pack a .44 magnum and, within an hour, be in New York City, surviving the subways.

The People's Republic of New Jersey gets short shrift, even from other Yankees. They may have seen the Berkshires of Massachusetts (which are beautiful...I keep a picture on my desk from our trip there last fall); but in all likelihood, they never got off the turnpike to see the rolling hills of Sussex County. The turnpike is a great way to get around during rush hour, but it is a terrible way to see The People's Republic of New Jersey.

Before she died, Grandma told me never to mention this (unless it was absolutely necessary), but my Great-Great Uncle Duke Haynes joined the Union Army in Pensacola back during "The Late Unpleasantness."

The family was always sort of shy about talking about Uncle Duke. They would fill us with stories about "The Late Unpleasantness," but Uncle Duke was always left out. I remember stories about General Lee and "The Charge up *Porkchop Hill*." About Bull Halsey and "The Battle of *Mobile Bay*." Oh, they were good stories. And even though the *South* won in the disagreement, we were always taught to be kind to Yankees—because Uncle Duke had tried his best to help them.

As I understand it, the South allowed the Union to retain its name—"The United States of America." The Confederate Nation dropped its name to join in with the larger whole as part of the agreement. As I understand it, the whole process was sort of a "leveraged buyout" maneuver.

Most of my relatives have served in the <u>Union</u> Navy. I did myself. My brother is still in the Union Navy Reserves, and my brother-in-law (who is a Yankee) also serves with the Union Navy. So, I appreciate one reader's allusions to "E Pluribus Unum" (one, out of many). It was a strong point which was absolutely correct.

OFF TO THE RACES

In New Jersey, there is a large horse racing complex called "The Meadowlands." There are fancy restaurants inside and computer-controlled betting windows. From the track, you can see the skyline of New York City. It is a beautiful place to go for dinner and to invest in the horses. Of course, if you were to go there to bet on them, that would be *sinful*. Being a cautious man, I went there to "invest" in them.

I had not attended a horse race since August 1965. I can remember the hot Saturday afternoon well. From that day forward, I believed myself banned from all race tracks forever.

Jesse Ellis and his family raised thoroughbred horses. Their farm was off Chumuckla Springs Road. Every Saturday in the summer, Jesse would have folks from all over come to his farm to race their stock against his. There was no betting, you understand, because a sinful nature was frowned upon in that part of the county.

One fall Saturday afterward, as I rode tall in the saddle on my gentle mare "Ripple," making tracks in the unpaved Chumuckla Springs Road, I crossed paths with a modest red diamondback rattlesnake. Following my usual inclination to collect snakes, I took Ripple to the side of the road and hitched her to a tree. I found a stick for snake catching and went about the business of capturing the venomous reptile. Danny Holt happened on the scene as he drove down the road. I asked for a lift to the Ellis Place, where I thought I might find a big jar or a sack. Danny was a year older than me and a good deal smarter. He offered a ride, but not inside the car. I could ride on the hood and I could pick Ripple up later.

Forgetting the sensitive nature of horses, I showed up at the races on the hood of Danny Holt's car with a live rattle-snake in my hands. I never saw such a wild frenzy of horses. Records would have been broken—had there been time to keep any—and if the horses had remained inside the race track. It took weeks to get some of them out of the swamps.

Needless to say, I was never invited back to the races. The snake fared even worse. It was sacrificed for a science project that Danny Ellis (Jesse's son) and I completed for biology class at school.

Fortunately for me, Jesse had not notified the Meadowlands of my previous behavior, and I was admitted to the New Jersey track without a search.

Up here they have what is called "harness racing." The horse pulls a little cart with a man in it. There is a special thrill to hear the bugle play, to watch the horses race, and to read the racing program as if you know what you are doing.

I *invested* two dollars in "Perry Noyd" in the first race, "Wide Load" and "Family Tree" in the third, and "Prince Lee Knight" in the fourth. Later, I threw away caution and began to *bet*.

After betting two dollars on "Vicarious Thrills" in the seventh, my wife stopped me. I had lost twenty dollars from my investments, and she did not approve of mortgaging the house to bet on "Little Lou Rain" in the eighth race.

"Little Lou Rain" won and paid ten to one. If I had bet on him, I could have retired to a life of idleness. (My wife questions that this is a "goal" since she believes me to be fairly idle already.) Anyway, idle hands lead to mischief. So maybe I would have become a broker and taken up *betting* on the stock market.

My wife will not allow me to carry more than a dollar fifty in my pocket. So I am considering selling my blood to get enough cash for my next investment. I have a hunch the horse named "Little Rattler" will be a big winner for me.

$$\$\$\$\$\$\$\$$

STARLIGHT EXPRESS

When you have an opportunity to visit New York City, you will want to see a Broadway Show. Granted, it will not be of the same quality as the high school plays presented in Santa Rosa County, but you will enjoy it just the same.

The plays at our school were normally produced by the Junior or Senior Class, under the direction of the teacher assigned to American Literature. Our teacher at Chumuckla was Mrs. Louise Driggers. We produced a play in both our Junior and Senior years. We were quite good. The plays brought in about as much money as we could earn with an afternoon car wash at "Pug Carnley's Grocery and Gas Station" in downtown Chumuckla.

My wife and I went into "The Pink Zone" (Manhattan, to those not familiar with color-coded state maps). We attended a matinee performance of "Starlight Express," a Broadway play that enjoyed a profitable run. Mrs. Driggers would have been proud of the performance. They were almost as good as her acne-plagued charges had been in 1966.

The story of the play, or musical, revolves around a train race. Diesel engines, electric engines and the hero, a steam engine, were the participants. The engines and the cars they pull were represented by people in costume who moved about the stage on roller skates. Of course, in the end, with the help of a mystical "Starlight Express," the Steam Engine wins the race. It is sort of musical version of "The Little Engine That Could."

We enjoyed the show. The roller skating performance was spectacular. My last experience with roller skates, at the Milton Roller Rink, left people askew on the floor with split lips, crushed fingers, and sore whereabouts. It wasn't my fault I couldn't control the direction of the skates. Nevertheless, I felt it prudent to avoid further contact with roller skate aficionados.

The performance of "Starlight Express" was a good one—a fun show to see. The stage effects were fantastically good—really spectacular. The actors skated on bridges suspended over the stage and across a smooth, undulating stage, curving through pathways that appeared almost impossible from the perspective of the audience.

Maybe you will visit New York City one day. And maybe you will see a Broadway Show. I hope so. But don't expect the same quality as the high school productions back home.

§§§§§§

PEARL GREY

After Queen Victoria lost her Prince Albert, she was always seen in 'pearl grey' gowns. The color was one that the prince had worn regularly. It was the Queen's way of showing an undying love for her prince.

If you have carefully viewed many *color* photographs of the era, you will have noticed that virtually everyone was keen on grey. And, pearl grey was just another shade of grey.

My maternal grandmother was named "Navy Victoria" in honor of the Queen, who was still living at the time of Grandma's birth in the late 19th century. At the time it was a popular notion to use a color in naming one's child. Thus Granny was given the name, "Navy." In mid 20th century, in honor of my grandmother, I was named "Victor," but no color was added to my name.

Pity the Grey family's son, born in 1872. His parents named him "Pearl" for the color of "respect" worn by Queen Victoria. It must have been a burdensome name. Can you imagine calling a boy "Pearl"? "Pearl Grey."

Pearl grew up to become a dentist. After several bountiful years, he took up writing. In 1939, following a successful career, he died.

Recently, I visited some people who knew him. Albert and Helen James Davis live in the old "Grey House," at the confluence of the Lackawaxen and Delaware Rivers in Pennsylvania. They maintain a small museum there, dedicated to remembering the achievements of Pearl, the ex-dentist.

Mrs. Davis's father, Colonel Alvah D. James, an explorer, befriended the dentist Pearl in New York City. He invited Grey to join him on a vacation in the Delaware River Valley. While there, in 1907, he introduced Grey to a retired buffalo hunter. The old plainsman took the aspiring writer West with him, where the Colonel hoped that Pearl would write a clear and inspiring description of scientific efforts to breed cattle with buffalo.

The idea never caught on very much. The colonel proved the idea, but not much came of the enterprise. Only recently have cattle breeders made serious attempts to promote "beefalo" again.

Pearl, though, had his first look at the American West. He was entranced by stories from people he met and by the things that he saw. He soon followed his experience with one novel, and then another—and more. In all, he completed more than fifty novels, and innumerable short stories. Over one hundred movies were based on his works. He practically invented the style of "The American Western."

I'm glad I had a chance to stop by the little museum and visit with Mr. and Mrs. Davis. But it is a good thing Pearl used his middle name when he signed his books.

If the museum had not been called "The Zane Grey Museum," I would never have thought to stop.

V

The Real World

"Somebody said we should get out and see 'the real world,' but it was right under our feet all the time."

"Philosophically, I am against nuclear arms. But there are occasions where, it seems to me, the use of an efficient, tactical, low-yield thermonuclear warhead could be of great benefit."

FORM 1040 AND THE TAXING LIFE

I first learned about paying Income Taxes when I was a Senior at Chumuckla High School. Chumuckla is a farm community in the far Western reaches of the Florida Panhandle. In the 1950s and 1960s, as prosperity found its way to Chumuckla, it became necessary to instruct the populace in the proper completion of an IRS Form 1040.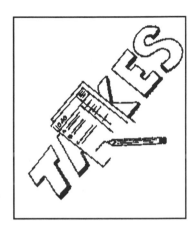

In 1966 this responsibility fell on my cousin, Margaret Campbell, who was the leading authority on taxes in our school. Cousin Margaret taught Home Economics and Family Living. Aside from teaching the art of making biscuits and cooking rice, her lot in life was to teach daydreaming teenagers the important facts of life—HOW TO FILE YOUR FEDERAL INCOME TAX.

It was not a popular subject. We much preferred the lectures on how reproduction occurs. Why do bees make honey, and why do birds build nests? (You know what I mean.)

Often, and deeply, I have regretted my inattention during the income tax lectures. Filling out all those forms is disgusting. In fact, however, the chore has not been done by me since my wife completed her masters degree in mathematics. It seems to me that such an advanced degree is a requirement to successfully complete the government forms we receive in the mail.

Not only does my wife complete the tax forms, she also cooks good biscuits and rice. On occasion, if she is too busy cleaning floors, I have had to pour my own milk for my artificially sweetened, artificially fortified, "Rambo Oat Puffies" breakfast cereal. Life is not so complicated as my Cousin Margaret thought it would be.

I have given a measure of thought to what my taxes pay for. Some of the things the government spends my money on seems a true waste. Some seem to be for real needs. I justify the government's seizure of my "disallowable income" by pretending that my portion goes to some good cause.

A good cause, for instance, would be aid to developing countries. Such help can decrease the level of poverty and ignorance in the world. One example is the rehabilitation of Ferdinand and Imelda Marcos, who would have been poor, despondent peasants were it not for the financial freedom they found through U.S. government aid. Using their own talents, and an "official" income of $1500 per month, the Marcos family in the Philippines built a personal fortune estimated at TEN BILLION DOLLARS.

Having studied at the Marcos School of Creative Investing, Baby Doc Duvalier, a poor orphan from Haiti, was able to amass upwards of HALF A BILLION DOLLARS.

It warms the heart to hear of success stories like these. Without my tax contributions, these people might never have found the good life.

I marvel at the amount of taxes I pay now. Sometimes, I think it is enough to control the political machines of half a dozen voting districts in Boston or Chicago. Some well-placed Federal grants can oil a lot of political machinery.

The Department of Defense is probably able to buy a complete toilet seat with my contribution.

There is waste though. For example, the government has spent money to build highways to North Dakota. Who is going to North Dakota? On the other hand, maybe North Dakotans are leaving.

The Navy spends tax dollars to buy new tires for jet aircraft. They would save a lot of money if they took the old ones to "Jay Tire and Recap Company" in Jay, Florida, and had them recapped.

They spend tax money to support colleges and universities. Do they think Americans are dumb or something? I think most Americans are pretty smart already.

They spend tax money to clean up air. They spend it to help poor people. The spend it to help sick people. They never seem to make any progress with all the money they spend on these projects.

They spend money on air traffic control, riot control, drug control, erosion control, and crime control. So how come everything seems out of control?

The money spent on defense to protect us from the Communists seems a good cause though. I have not been shot at by a Communist in several years now.

₷₷₷₷₷₷

AND THE RAIN FALLS

Thomas "Two Toe" Turnipseed (who was a near world-class master in the game of barefoot mumblety peg) once told me a gem of wisdom I shall never forget.

"Vic," he said, "When it is cold and raining. When the sun won't shine. When the dirt gets dirty. When the climate is unkind. When this happens, it seems some people manage to be situated by a warm fire. They have a roof over their heads, a cup of hot coffee, and a remote-control TV to escape from the weather. Other people are standing in the wind, chilled to the bone with mud up to their knees."

"Life ain't fair," he said. "Often as not, it just happens to be where you are standing at the time."

The opposite situation, he explained, was also true. In other words, when the sun shines and the birds sing in harmony, some will enjoy it all. Others will miss out just because they are not there at that particular time.

I'm not sure what all this means. Maybe he means it is too bad life is not more fair. How come Sigmund G. Pimrod III seems to get all the sunshine and Lester "L. L." Lintrap seems to get all the rain?

I met a young fellow in my company recently who told me how his family *struggled* when he was a boy. They made every effort to conserve money and preserve the family income. He explained how each of the children in the family was assigned a portion of the *family stock portfolio*. They each bought and sold shares of stock, learning the conservative principles of money management from their father. The children picked the stocks.

I stared in awe at this fellow for a moment. His gold cufflinks flashed brightly in my eyes.

Then I explained to him that I, too, was allowed to pick things as a child. Pop would let us young'uns pick okra and tomatoes as well a butterbeans—and even cotton.

"Why, you old *stock picker*, you," I remarked, "You and I have so much in common."

Besides whether life is fair or not, I suppose, also depends on your perspective.

I thought I might sum up "Two Toe's" philosophy with a simple, one liner. So, I have, after much deliberation, come up with this.

"The rain falls on the just and the unjust alike."

You can quote me on that if you wish.

$$\text{\$\$\$\$\$\$}$$

FRESH BAIT

Spring is very near. I can tell because I have just received fourteen catalogs in the mail. All except the "Burpee Seed Catalog" touts fishing lures. Every department store I have been in for the past week has a new display of rods, reels, and angling paraphernalia.

I get carried away with the fancy lures, the special line, the hydrodynamic sinkers, and the high-impact plastic tackle boxes.

It wasn't always that way. I used to fish with a cane pole and some tangled nylon, 136-lb test-weight fishing line. The cork was the size of a basketball, and a rusty size 5/0 hook was tied to the far end of the line. The hook was an ideal size to comfortably hold three mutilated earthworms taken from the moist earth under the old camphor tree in Grandma's back yard. Occasionally, I caught a fish.

Today, the demands of modern angling require the care and feeding of a large retinue of anything-but-life-like, glitzy, plastic worm and fish imitators. Some rattle. Some dive. Some wiggle. Some dance and twist. All of them attract trees.

Live bait is passé.

In the "sports section" of the local department store, a clerk greeted me and slapped me on the back. "What a friendly place," I thought. He told me a few wild stories about local fishing holes and led me to a wall covered with the latest models in shiny new lures.

"This one will cause aggressive strikes from overweight bass," said the self-confessed expert.

"I'll take two—uh, make that three," I offered.

The clerk then introduced me to the reel specialist, who rattled off the names of spinning reels made in Korea, Taiwan, Japan, Germany, and Yugoslavia. The names spilled off his lips as if written in the poetry of springtime. Some of the equipment was special-ordered from Maine.

"I'll take that one," I said, pointing to the one with the aerodynamic shape and the unique magnum drag system complete with a quick-adjust power lever. He handed me a box with the reel inside and then introduced me to the tackle box specialist.

"Gotta have worm-proof plastic, mister," he said. "The plastic worms will destroy the average cheap tackle box."

After discussing my needs with a number of specialists, I left the store with enough ammunition to launch a major attack on the U.S. fish population.

When my wife saw my new supply of technical equipment to address the rites of spring, she smiled a bit. Then she turned me around and pulled off the sign that clung to my jacket.

The sign read, "LIVE BAIT."

§§§§§§§

NEVER WITHOUT A KNIFE

I was told I could have a knife as soon as I was old enough to handle the responsibility. Maturity and depth of character were key requirements, according to Pop.

I wanted a knife of my own because Jim Bowie had one at the Alamo. All of the grownup men that I knew had one. Most kids over the age of six had one. It was embarrassing <u>not</u> to have a knife. It was akin to wearing short pants when all the other guys were wearing long pants. To be without a knife was to be *naked*.

My first sharp instrument all my own was an axe. The folks had built our house with a fireplace that consumed logs imported from the back forty. I used a child-size axe to trim the smaller limbs from the trees, and Pop completed the job with a man-size axe.

Having gained maturity with the axe, I was graduated to a scalpel. My Uncle Olyn, the veterinarian, taught us how to use a scalpel or a razor blade to neuter young pigs and calves. It was a job that required speed, skill, and depth of character. A slow surgeon is not appreciated when his assistants are trying to hold a 400-lb calf that could  kick a hole in the side of your head and has good reason for doing it.

After some maturity from chopping wood, and some depth of character from working with farm animals, I earned my first knife. It was a time to be proud. Having a knife bespoke responsibility.

It was a fishing knife with a leather handle and a leather scabbard. I scaled some fish with it and cut some fishing line, but it did not become a constant companion.

The teachers and Foster "Two-Toe" Turnipseed's mom did not appreciate the large, sheathed knife I wore at my side. "Two Toe" was a master at mumblety peg. He would never flinch, no matter how close the challenger's knife came to his bare foot. Thus his nickname. Soon thereafter, I graduated to a more discreet pocket knife.

It was a Barlow knife and it came in handy for innumerable tasks, like cleaning out from under my fingernails and cutting Dick Tracy's Crime Stoppers Notebook from the Sunday Paper. Occasionally, after dipping it in a solution of Lysol and warm water, it was used to perform radical surgery on male pigs and bull calves.

If ever attacked by pirates, wild Indians, or a rabid bobcat, I would be prepared. My knife and I could repel the attack. I guess, deep down, I still expect there is potential for an attack like that. After all, I live in New Jersey

So to this day, I carry a pocket knife. I am not fully dressed without one. And the knife is still handy for cleaning fingernails and cutting comics out of the Sunday Paper. The thrill of mumblety peg is not the same, however, since the regulations at my company require us to wear steel-toed safety shoes to play the game.

$$\oint\oint\oint\oint\oint\oint\oint$$

THE REDEEMING VALUE OF SPORTS

I am not much on sports. Some might accuse me of being a Communist when it comes to sports—or at the very least, un-American. Ever since Gary Lockett replaced me in right field for the Chumuckla Little League baseball team, I figured sports were not in the cards for me. Simply because I couldn't catch a ball or throw one straight and true, they pulled me off the field. I started wearing glasses soon after that, but it was too late; I had already grown to dislike the agony of defeat.

It wasn't always that way. In 1959 I felt true pride in the Chumuckla football team. I was in Mrs. Dovie Stewart's Fourth Grade class, so I wasn't old enough for the team. But I used to go to the home games with my brother Jim and Pop.

I recall one game against the Jay Royals. I think it was Jack Caraway who broke through the line at the Jay 20-yard line and rushed up the far side of the field. He was surrounded by fellow "Indians" like Jeffrey Cotton, Jerry Kilpatrick, Tommy Reynolds, Atwood Kimbrough, and Ray Lowerey. The Jay defense crumbled. Jack scored a touchdown after an 80-yard run. It was exciting! Chumuckla (Pop. 300) actually scored a touchdown against the

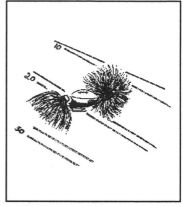

cosmopolitan team from Jay (Pop. 750). We had really nice cheerleaders, but we lost the game anyway.

By 1961 football was no longer in our school program. The equipment and uniforms, donated by the Whiting Field Navy team, were worn out. There were not enough students to make up a team. The defensive team and the offensive team were the same. With one injury, the game was ended.

Jeffrey Cotton tells me that he can't remember ever winning a game in two years. So in time, you understand, I lost interest in football as well as baseball. Basketball did not appeal to me because it seemed to me all you did was sweat a lot and run around out of breath. The cheerleaders were really nice, though.

My interest in football was rekindled recently. Some friends took Karen and me to see Army play Wake Forest at the U.S. Military Academy at West Point. Wake Forest is a North Carolina school noted for its theological seminary. West Point, of course, is known as the school General Custer attended. He graduated next to last in his class. His academic record finally caught up with him at the Little Big Horn River in Montana.

154

At West Point the "tailgate" picnic has been elevated to a fine art. Tasty foods—served with table appointments of silver candelabrum, fresh flowers, fine crystal, and linen—are enjoyed among the surrounding hills. Brilliant fall foliage adds perfection to the outing. I suppose if you have to have football to have tailgate picnics, the sport has redeeming qualities.

As for the game, one would have expected the Army Knights to thoroughly trounce the Wake Forest Deacons. However, the Deacons beat the Knights 48 to 14. We can only hope the Army will manage a better defense should the "Red Hoard" mount an attack on the free world.

The female "Cheer Coordination Specialists" were really nice, though.

$$\oint\oint\oint\oint\oint\oint\oint$$

NAMES HAVE BEEN CHANGED

The names have been changed to protect the innocent. Nobody was really at fault. Probably, not even the dog. If the dog had not been overly fond of fresh eggs and if the hen's nests had been enclosed, rather than under the house and inside the abandoned hay baler, "Ol' Scum" would have never become an "egg sucker."

Unfortunately for Ol' Scum, egg-sucking dogs received little respect in our county. To be called an "egg sucker" was about as bad a name as the meanest and most sinister criminal of the time could merit.

Most everybody knew that Ol' Scum was an egg sucker. The super glossy coat of fur sported by the blue-tick hound was a clue to any observant passerby. About the only one that didn't know was Mr. Peapod, who owned the dog. Rudyard "Rud" Peapod and his wife, Martha, lived in a farmhouse, not a half mile from "Two-Toe" Turnipseed (who in later life became a soldier of fortune).

Nobody had the heart to tell Rud that his dog was an egg sucker. People just don't speak ill of another person's dog in our part of the county—at least not to his face.

The story now begins.

"Two-Toe" had been experimenting over the summer with pet horseflies. Entomologists, according to my friend Lynn DuBose, call them "Tabanids." It distinguishes them from the more nasty versions of flies we are accustomed to swatting with newspapers. "Two-Toe" had captured several of the blood-sipping flies from his sunburned shoulders while swimming in the clear water at Sand Creek.

Our fledgling scientist tied a sewing thread around the neck of the fly and allow it to roam about—but never more than five feet away. There were times when our creative chap would harness up to six horseflies in teams and put on a show for the giggling girls at the swimming hole.

The idea came to "Two-Toe" in a flash of unmitigated genius. He would tie a horsefly to Ol' Scum's collar and drive the dog insane. This, he surmised, would be sufficient punishment for the crime of egg sucking.

It was just chance that "TT" sneaked up on the sleeping dog one evening just as Mr. Peapod finished reading a chapter in the book, "To Kill A Mockingbird." In that chapter,

Addicus, the man who later *starred in the role of Gregory Peck* in the movie version of the book, was forced to shoot a "mad" dog.

When Ol' Scum woke up, he was pestered by an obese and overly active Tabanid. He knew it was a Tabanid and not one of those nasty houseflies because it had just taken a bite out of his left ear and sucked a quart of high-cholesterol blood out of his yard-egg-primed body.

Scum was yelping and jumping and snapping at the fly. The fly couldn't get away, but the dog couldn't catch it either. Scum snapped and jumped and yelped for some time before Rud noticed the commotion. When he saw the dog, Scum was foaming at the mouth and twisting his body in the air with wild fury.

"Martha, git the gun, Ol' Scum's gone and got the rabies." Mr. Peapod quickly worked himself into a frightful state of anxiety, assuming he must now star as *Addicus* (playing the role of Gregory Peck in "To Kill A Mockingbird") and save our community from the terror of a "mad" dog.

The dog survived only because Ol' Man Peapod was an awful shot. But from that day on, Scum was so nervous he had to be cared for like a baby, and egg sucking was a thing of the past in that part of the county—at least for a time.

$$\oint\oint\oint\oint\oint\oint\oint$$

I AM NOT NOW, NOR HAVE I EVER BEEN

The recent brouhaha over the nominations for the Supreme Court have prompted me to bring out all the skeletons in my closet. I do not wish to leave any surprises for the President, should he turn to me in desperation in a last-ditch effort to find a suitable judge.

First, I want it clearly known that I have never smoked marijuana. This is hard for some people to believe. I have been the object of numerous quizzical looks and comments of disbelief when I mention this truth. But, it is a fact.

"How can you have attended college in the sixties and seventies and be a Vietnam Veteran and never have tried drugs?" they ask. It is almost as if they expect me to apologize. "Sorry, I guess I was just in the wrong places at the wrong time; it just happened."

At last count, I have recorded seven people of my generation, who, like me, never smoked a "joint" or ran naked through a parking lot. We seven just did not make good news copy. We were very dull people.

But, I was no angel either.

I have smoked rabbit tobacco, rolled up in newspaper. The little weed is fairly common. When you're thirteen years old and "Pug" Carnley (of Pug Carnley's Grocery and Gulf Service Station) knows who you are and knows your folks, you'll have a difficult time paying cash for a pack of Camel cigarettes.

When the rabbit tobacco was scarce, we used corn silk. We rolled the silk up in a strip of shucks. It was better when the silk was already dry. It took a blow torch to keep the green stuff lit.

I once used up a box of "Diamond" brand kitchen matches just for the pleasure of smoking a completely green corn silk cigarette.

When I was in the Navy, I tried a pipe. The pipe and loose tobacco would fall all over the deck as the ship rolled from side to side. At last, I gave up trying to smoke anything—except an occasional turkey on a gas grill.

For the Congressional inquiry, I will admit to having torn off the materials display tag on a pillow one time. The shame of the action prevents me from doing it again. The notice on the tag read, "DO NOT REMOVE UNDER PENALTY OF FEDERAL LAW." I am the kind of guy that looks guilty whether I did anything to feel guilty about or not. I could feel the accusing glances of "law-abiding" citizens for weeks following the criminal "tag" episode.

On more than one occasion, I have experienced the hormonal rush of passion that romanticists associate with myocardial pulsations. But, Mr. President, even Ex-President Jimmy Carter admitted to that weakness.

Lastly, and for the record, I am guilty of using the "EXPRESS" checkout lane to purchase seventeen items when the posted limit was ten or under.

Now, all is out in the open. When the President wishes to tap my experience for public service, my record and my conscience are clear. The misdemeanors of my past are aired here for all to see.

So, why aren't the phones ringing?

$$\$\$\$\$\$\$\$$

TECHNOLOGY IS ONLY A TEMPORARY OBSTACLE

"Nuke it!" That's what my wife says when she cooks something in her microwave. She loves her microwave.

So did Joyce Stewart, Paul's wife. Joyce and Paul live in New York. This is not the New York of strange tribal customs that lies on the seaward end of the Hudson River. This is the New York situated within a mile radius of the New Bethel Baptist Church—a few miles north of Chumuckla and a few miles south of Bernie Diamond's Store. Forty Acre Pond is about three miles southeast.

Joyce works as a dental hygienist with Dr. Hudon in Milton. Paul works with heavy equipment for a big contractor in Pensacola. They have a nice family and a long heritage in Santa Rosa County.

Paul is normally a very stable, predictable, dependable sort of fellow. He has a calm disposition. Even Vietnam didn't set him off. "The EPISODE," as I see it, started with the diet. If he hadn't been on a diet, he wouldn't have been so hungry.

Paul returned after one of those "awful" days at work. Joyce was working late, cleaning somebody's third mandibular molar because he did not floss his teeth regularly. She left a chicken in the microwave, however. A timer was set to cook the bird in time for Paul's supper. A note informed Paul that supper was in the oven.

If he hadn't been on a diet, he wouldn't have been so hungry. The "nuked" chicken behind the locked microwave oven door wouldn't have looked so irresistible. If it had not looked so irresistible, Paul wouldn't have been upset when the door did not open.

160

If he had not been upset over the locked door, he would not have verbally abused the engineer who placed the fuse for the oven in a place that requires two hours of careful disassembly for replacement. And, he also would not have verbally assaulted the "Consumer Safety Council" for requiring microwave doors to be locked when the appliance is in use. If he had not verbally attacked every technological advance since the dawn of plastic, he might have avoided the flare of temper that attracted a ball peen hammer to his clenched fist.

Pulse accelerating, eyes intense, and choking with rage, Paul murdered the invalid microwave. He beat the door off with the hammer, grabbed the now-cold chicken by a tender cooked leg, and slung the dead fowl from the kitchen porch for the culinary pleasure of his surprised and delighted dogs.

The dogs, under the heated glare of a desperate Paul, latched onto the morsel and moved carefully backward, tails between legs, to the side of the house, where they could avoid the anger of a man on a diet with no hope of satisfaction.

The last time I saw Paul, he was as calm as ever. He seemed to have both his weight and his temper under control.

Joyce is just happy the children—LuJuan, Douglas, and Emily—were not at home during "The EPISODE" and were not exposed to the dark side of modern living. I could detect in her voice, however, the desire for a new microwave oven.

$$\text{\$\$\$\$\$\$\$}$$

THE CITY CAFE

For those who are more accustomed to the cosmopolitan restaurants of the metropolitan areas of Milton and Gulf Breeze, let me suggest a fine dining experience in the northern end of our county.

First, you need a reason to go to Jay. There are many. Check on your Farm Bureau Insurance records and possibly order a new set of mud grip tires for your truck. Stop in at the Jay Co-Op to buy a new float valve for your livestock watering trough. Get a block of red trace mineral salt while you are there; or better yet, get a couple of fifty-pound sacks of medicated minerals. Don't forget the tube of grease for the grease gun. You don't want to leave your farm equipment out all winter without properly servicing it.

Now, you are almost ready for breakfast. If it is Tuesday, it is sale day at the Jay Livestock Barn, so before you go to The City Cafe (where parking is at a premium), take time to drop off your livestock trailer at The Sale Barn, beyond the Peanut Warehouse. Now drive to The City Cafe and park the truck.

If you are lucky, it will be raining. Not a drizzle, but not so hard that it would wash the dog out from under the house either. The mood of Jay is much better suited to rain. Rain attracts more of the local citizenry to the cafe for coffee and breakfast.

By this point in your quest for a culinary experience and native atmosphere, it's about 9 a.m. Smell the air. Take note of how clean it is. Now, step out of your truck and move confidently to the door under The City Cafe sign. The odor of frying bacon wraps itself around you and snatches you inside the door.

Here at The City Cafe, you can have a scrambled egg sandwich, all the coffee you want, a free paper with national news and livestock markets, and local rumors embellished with moral philosophy. You may also hear the latest "true life" hunting story, told by "Buddy" Harrison, followed by a lively debate between "Shine" Carden and Curt Cannon over the relative virtues of bipartisan support for the price of tea in China. All this will cost only eighty cents.

If you do not have a truck, or a livestock trailer, or a John Deere cap, you'll perhaps miss some of the atmosphere. But go anyway; you'll be welcome. That's the way it is in Jay.

You can always buy the truck (try to get one with a stainless steel dog box) and livestock trailer later. The cap comes free with the tractor.

«   »

Etiquette at the City Cafe

The linoleum on the floor is worn down. A few fellows at the long table in the back look up from their morning conversation and gaze at you with modest suspicion.

Take your John Deere cap off and say, "How y'all doin?" Smile.

Probably some of the Hunter boys or a Godwin or two are at that table. Maybe a Gavin. They'll wonder who you are for awhile. That's part of the atmosphere. The Jones boys may glance your way as they head out the door. They've been there since 7:30. "Junior" Smith and Carlos Gavin have to leave now, too. The tractor business is waiting. "D." Allen left earlier. He says he has to work for a living.

One may ask you, "Say, ain't you D.B.'s boy?"

Answer the man, "Naw, I'm R.T.'s boy (or whoever, even if you are from Iowa and they don't know who R.T. is). Are you one of the Lowery boys?"

One of them is bound to be one of the Lowery boys. It does not matter that they may be over fifty years old. They are still "boys." When they reach the age of seventy, a kind of knighthood is bestowed; then, maybe, you call them "Mister."

The fellow with T. T. ("Two Toe") Turnipseed at the corner table is Junior Wade. He has a grin full of teeth and a Bic pen in his hand. Just above their heads, on the wall, is a Liberty National Insurance calendar. It features a large, colorful map of Alabama.

The two are talking about the insurance policy Junior sold "Two Toe" at this same table five years ago. This morning Junior will buy "Two Toe's" breakfast. He'll put the eighty cents on his expense account.

Mattie Brae, the manager, motions you to sit at the table by the wall, under a drooping fishing net.

That's Millie standing over you with a pencil in one hand and a pad of receipts in the other. She'll say, "Can I help you?"

And, you'll say "Yes ma'am. I believe I'd like to have two eggs over easy, with grits, and toast, and a cup of coffee. Oh, and some bacon too, please ma'am."

And she'll say, "Okay hon, but if you like sausage, we have some of the very best sausage you ever tasted. We get our smoked sausage from Mr. Jim Rheam in Cobbtown. You should have some."

"Okay ma'am," you say, "I believe I'll have some of that sausage. Thank you, ma'am."

B. D. Hendricks speaks up from the table next to you, "You gonna like that sausage, boy, it's real good."

Louis Frank Smith, nodding his head in agreement, says, "Yup."

J. Lee Campbell enters the cafe now. His grandson, Wesley Roberts is with him. Wesley is six years old and seems to appreciate this vision of America that will be implanted in his young mind. They have rushed a bit to escape the rain. The door slams behind them.

"How you doin' Miss Mattie," he says, as she points to a table by the wall.

The cafe is real, the people are real, the sausage is excellent. On this morning in The City Cafe in Jay, Florida, you are going to enjoy your breakfast—and you will be proud to be an American.

You'll finish your coffee, pay your "tab," and head back to the livestock auction, where you will want to bid on some yearling angus heifers for your herd. That is another story.

« »

Politics in the City Cafe

The reason there is so much political turmoil in Jay is because the town lies, geographically speaking, right smack in the middle of four "hotbeds" of government intrigue. The patrician politics of Milton, Florida, are due south. Andalusia, Alabama, lies northeast and anchors the "Good Old Boy" network. Brewton, Alabama, sizzles with activity due north of Jay. Century, Florida, a cauldron of Alabama sympathizers, is only nine miles west.

In many ways, Jay is like the Jerusalem of old. It is the crossroads of trade. It is the meeting place of minds. It is where the conquerors pass through on the way to conquer (Class Triple C basketball teams). It is where you can stop in at The City Cafe and get all the latest news, a cup of coffee, two eggs over easy, and a side order of grits and bacon for only a buck twenty-nine.

When J. C. Marshall pulled his rig over and stopped in front of The City Cafe, he had both coffee and politics on his mind. He left the truck idling. The sign on the door of the fuel truck read "R. J. Stuckey, Jr., Inc., Century, Florida." I could hear the diesel engine hummma hummma hummm when he opened the door to the cafe and stepped inside. The door squeaked and slammed shut. It was quiet.

—For only a second.

"Did y'all see where Ol' Bush done won for president?" J.C. baited the audience. "Y'all gonna be sorry. I <u>know</u> y'all voted Republican." Another cast. Like a fisherman casting a fluorescent plastic grub rigged with a hammered brass jig spinner attached with small-diameter high-strength, supple monofilament line to a quick, fine reel with micro-precision worm-shaft oscillation held fast to a graphite rod, J.C. was looking for a "big mouth." "Him annat Quayle gonna break the bank. Fowreners gonna own the country."

I bit.

"Well, I'm not too concerned," I said. "I got a job with a foreign company."

"Ol' Reagan got us nine point two *trillyun* dollars in debt," said J.C. "Somebody gonna have to pay furrit. And, not onlyat, they run eighty thousand farmers outa business in the midwest."

166

By now the other patrons in the cafe were focused on the activity at my table. They were all farmers. At the table to my left, the discussion about the correct hitch pin for a cotton wagon stopped in mid-sentence.

"Eighty-thousand farmers—<u>poof</u>!" he emphasized.

"Well," I said, "you know for every ten thousand farmers that go out of business in the midwest, the farmers here get two percent more for their crops because of less competition."

Rube Ard relaxed and started chewing his biscuit again.

"You gonna be sorry. I voted for that Dukaky fellow even though he has a funny name. He had a plan to save the farmers," he answered.

"Well it seems he was going to cut defense, and he didn't believe in the death penalty, and he seemed too liberal for most folks," I offered.

"Now me, I'm a <u>Democrat</u>, but I ain't no *liberal*. No sir, NOT a liberal. Not me. Okay your Bush feller has some good points. I can talk both ways (Democrat or Republican), but you still gonna be sorry."

J. C. had finished his cup of coffee now and was halfway out the door. D. Allen yelled from the back of the room. "Hey! J. C.! Florida Gators gonna whip the tar outa Alabama this year."

"Ain't got time to argue politics with you buncha Republicans. I'm working. Gotta go." The door slammed; the truck engine revved up. J. C. was on the road to Andalusia.

National politics get major attention at The City Cafe.

$$\oint\oint\oint\oint\oint\oint$$

SEX AND THE SINGLE WEEVIL

The "Weevil Queens" are out early every day, before daylight, to stalk the wild weevils. Surely, those of you who are still breathing have noticed the bright green "jugs" staked out around cotton fields all over the county. These are weevil traps.

The USDA project, headed by Ken Pierce, a native Texan, and Bob Hulett, a native Arkansan, is designed to control the infamous Boll Weevil through reduced applications of pesticides.

The weevil traps are colored the exact shade of green that discriminating weevils prefer. They are set out on stakes that are the right shape and size to make weevils feel "at home on the stalk." Even the exact height of the trap above ground is guaranteed to make any weevil feel comfortable.

As a final lure, the traps are doused in "girl weevil perfume," a sort of "Beet'el No. 5" that drives boy weevils into an uncontrollable display of affection. Scientists call this type of "bug perfume" a pheromone, which is a type of hormone animals produce. The pheromone acts much like a perfume to attract the opposite sex. Pheromones, as another example, explain why gentlemen pigs like lady pigs.

Once the weevil is in the trap, his life as a free weevil is over. The next (and last) face he sees is likely to be one of the "Boll Weevil Queens" who are employed by the USDA to collect the hapless, love-struck bugs. Some of the "Boll Weevil Queens" in our county are Donna Ellis, Stephanie Godwin, Kitty Hatfield, and Helen Davis. There are also "Boll

Weevil Kings," like Timmy Russell. These people check the traps, of which there are, on average, one per acre of cotton. The bugs are delivered to the USDA, where they are counted, numbered, and statistically analyzed. Lula May Hunter coordinates the battle plans from the USDA Office in Jay.

When traps from a particular cotton field are producing as many as three weevils a day, it may be time to spray the field with malathion, one of the most innocuous insecticides available. Without the weevil traps, farmers would spray much more toxic insecticides in greater quantities and more often, because they could never be sure just how large the boll weevil crop was.

So, not only is the cotton boll weevil kept under control, but the use of toxic insecticides is kept to a minimum. Eventually, says Mr. Pierce, our county can expect results similar to those in North Carolina, where the program has been in effect for several years. This past month, the North Carolina boll weevil traps yielded only two weevils on 97,000 acres of cotton.

When I last looked, Copeland Griswold was hard at work, pulling a four-row cultivator behind his John Deere 2640. He drove from one end of the cotton field to the other, and he seemed confident the little green jugs would make the sex life of the single weevil a disappointing proposition.

There may be another economic benefit to this weevil-trapping business. Sources from Jay report an increase in the demand for boll weevil pelts. Some of the "Boll Weevil Queens" are skinning the little beetles, tanning their pelts, and shipping them to New York City where, I am told, fashion designers include them in all manner of clothing—coats, shoes, and handbags.

If the market for boll weevil pelts explodes, we may have to discard the weevil control program and grow cotton for the express purpose of feeding the voracious insects. "COMING SOON TO FASHION STORES NEAR YOU...*Full-length ranch weevil coats, made of perfectly matched hand-sewn boll weevil pelts. Quality insured by Floyd's of Chumuckla.*"

§§§§§§§

VI

The Class Reunion

"I hugged them and hugged them. They never let me hug them
when I was in high school with them. I waited 20 years for the
fantasy to become reality."

THE CLASS OF 1967 FINDS A HISTORY

In 1955 a group of six-year-old kids began their formal education at Chumuckla School in Santa Rosa County, Florida.

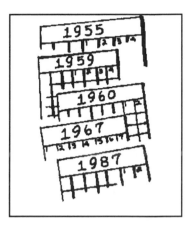

Our school was a little corner of the U.S.A. where history was something we read about in books. Events happened elsewhere and were printed in the newspapers. Our little class attended school with the firm belief that <u>all</u> history happened to other people—never to us.

Elvis was just beginning to hit it big in 1955. He has been in the news ever since—even more since he died. In 1956 the Federal Government began building what we know today as the "Interstate Highway System." In 1958 America launched its first satellite into space. Alaska and Hawaii became states in 1959.

In 1960, a U2 "Spy Plane" was shot down over Russia. In 1961 we lost a friendly Cuba to the communists when we failed to join the "Battle of The Bay of Pigs." We almost had a war of nuclear proportions with the U.S.S.R. in 1962 because of the unfriendly missiles being set up in Cuba. In that year, bomb shelters became big business.

In 1963 we began our 9th year of school. One day in November, we gathered in the gymnasium to hear our school principal, Mr. Temple, tell us that the President of the United States of America had been shot and killed.

Two U.S. Navy ships were fired on by unfriendly boats in the Gulf of Tonkin in 1964. The "Gulf of Tonkin Incident" sparked a massive buildup of U.S. troops in a place called Vietnam. We were in the 10th grade.

By 1967, our little band of students, mildly insulated until then from the events of the time, were primed to be participants in history.

Vietnam became a place we could readily find on any map of the world. We participated in the draft; supported the first effort to put a junkyard on the moon; helped make "baby boomer" economics become more than theory; and lived through oil shortages, oil surpluses, employment, unemployment, marriages, divorces, children, deaths of family and friends, and the farm crisis.

The Class of 1967 has experienced all these things and more.

Of course, it took more that just our twenty or so members to bring about the oil shortage. And we did not lose Vietnam all by ourselves. We had some help. Some of our fellow citizens from Chumuckla and, I think, Allentown, Cobbtown, Munson, Jay, Pea Ridge, and Milton were involved along with us.

We witnessed the Two Hundredth Anniversary of the our Country. In 1987 we celebrated the Two Hundredth Anniversary of the Constitution of The United States of America.

We the people. That's us. The Class of 1967. We are gaining experience through the living and making of history.

$$\phi\phi\phi\phi\phi\phi\phi$$

A HUGGING FRENZY AT THE REUNION

The class reunion was well under way. Fewer than twenty students made up the class in 1967. Yet nearly a dozen of my former classmates were there with their spouses. Now we took up conversations that had ended two decades ago. Could it perhaps have been only last week instead of twenty years?

I was impressed with the maturity of my classmates. The "world wise," daring, but innocent, boys of 1967 were now grizzled, surefooted, realists. I shook their hands and renewed a bond we had shared long, long ago—in a galaxy far, far away.

The unsure, pretty girls of 1967 had become radiant, purposeful, and beautiful women. I hugged them. And I hugged them. And I thoroughly enjoyed it.

I didn't make it public then, but at one time or another, I was in love with each of the women in my class.

In the 2nd Grade, I had a crush on Martha Walther. Martha's daddy was a school teacher. Rumor had it that "Plug," as he was called, cooked and ate several small boys who bothered his daughters. Once I heard that, my romantic intentions for Martha were placed on hold.

In the 5th Grade, I fell in love with Rhonda Enfinger. I kissed her on the cheek once in class. Our teacher, Mr. Williams, saw me do it. He took me to the storage room beside the 3rd Grade classroom and paddled me for unlicensed romance. That romance died a painful death.

Then, I fell in love with Brenda Ard. I put our initials inside my leather jacket as proof of my devotion. The other guys made a lot of fun of my romantic notions. They just did not understand. My love for Brenda became a casualty of 5th-Grade peer pressure.

In the 6th Grade, I had a crush on a girl named Cathy Bates. Once aware of my intentions, she left our school. Patsy Harris followed Cathy into my heart, but Patsy tuned me out.

By 7th Grade, all the girls were bigger than the boys and would only give serious thought to upper classmen—the more mature sophomores, juniors, and seniors. I tried talking to them, but I stammered.

Nancy Lowery was a beauty. She was soon snagged by an older "man." Carol Cook was a looker. She too found more pleasant company. Karen Hatfield, like all those Hatfield girls, made my heart go thumpity thump. Even she fell for an older man.

I especially admired my cousin, Faye Campbell. I think, though, there is something illegal about being in love with your cousin. To avoid prison, I simply admired her from afar.

Dorothy Steadham left me tongue-tied. Pamela Patterson and her twin sister, Paula, left me speechless. They all left me alone.

As I look at pictures in our old yearbook, I can understand their behavior. If you see pictures of me then, you will see a 112-pound nerd. Time has been kind to me; now, I am a 187-pound nerd.

I surely enjoyed hugging all those wonderful women from my high school class. They were very polite to permit my hugging frenzy. I felt much better, in light of all my romantic struggles.

None of their husbands threatened me or laid a hand on me either. I was a bit concerned with Pamela Patterson Butler's husband, Jimmie, though. He is eight feet-*sixteen inches* tall and weighs 373 pounds-*19 ounces*, or so it seemed.

I am told hugging is therapeutic. My wife, who was unable to attend the reunion, also agrees that hugging is therapeutic. However, she wants to be there while the medicine is administered. I bet she'll come to our next reunion.

ƒƒƒƒƒƒƒ

A RUDE AWAKENING

About a dozen of the former students showed up along with five teachers. It was the 20th reunion of the Chumuckla High School Class of 1967. Most of us met again for the first time since leaving school two decades past. Fewer than twenty people were in the final class. Perhaps as many as fifty were a part of us at one time or another in our twelve years of school.

After a period of reintroductions, family updates, and telling tales on one another, we became philosophical. What was it that made our time a special time? And what event was it that robbed us of youthful innocence to give us our first cruel look at the real world?

We each reviewed the event that provided our own, personal rude awakening. To the classmate (or spouse) with the worst experience, we would provide a certificate for the worst "rude awakening."

Rhonda Enfinger Forte said "It was having a child. This woke me up to the real world."

Brenda Ard Kelley said, for her, it was raising a family.

Pamela Patterson Butler and her twin, Paula, said they thought their awakening came was when they married. Pamela's husband, Jimmie, said he was not sure Pamela was awake to this day.

Junior said, "It was the first hour of the first class of the first week of my first year at college. The professor said, 'Look to your left and look to your right. Chances are the people you see there will not be here next year.' I was in an aisle seat, and the guy to my right was staring a hole in me!"

For some, the rude awakening was the letter they received in the mail from the Department of Defense which began, "Greetings..." and ordered them to show up for their draft appointment with the U.S. Army.

Paul Stewart said it was Vietnam. In all, thirty percent of our class served in Vietnam: Paul, Jerry, Benny Enfinger, Preston Carroll, and me.

Jerry Kelley said it was Vietnam for one year, then Vietnam for another year, and then Vietnam for a third year. Jerry is wide awake now.

In the end, we voted on the rudest of rude awakenings.

It was a close vote. "Raising a family" was tied with "Vietnam again and again" when Jerry Kelley threw his vote to Brenda, his wife and mother of their two children. Jerry said Vietnam and raising families have a much in common, especially when it comes to battle fatigue.

In the end, we forced Jerry to accept the award for "Most Rude Awakening."

I think he deserved it.

$$\oint\oint\oint\oint\oint\oint\oint$$

VII

A Global View

"Really, the people in other countries are exactly the same as we are—only they are different."

ADVANCE AUSTRALIA FAIR

I remember when, in 1964, my 9th Grade teacher left for Australia. He liked the country so much, he made his life there. I never saw Mr. Dennis Moore of Marion, Alabama, again.

In that same year, he taught school in the island province of Tasmania, Australia. While there, he offered the names of his former students as potential "pen pals." A fellow named Lloyd Robson, from the town of Stanley, wrote me and asked whether I wanted to correspond. I did. A fast and enduring friendship developed.

We have continued writing to one another at least twice a year for twenty-three years. I know his country; he knows mine. I know his "Mum" Betty, sisters Lynette and Lee, and his brother Dennis. His father died a few years ago. Lloyd knows my family. If I had to pick another country as a permanent home, I would choose his country. I would choose his island—Tasmania.

Lloyd's town depends mostly on thriving fishing and farming industries. Based on Lloyd's descriptions, the town and the people are much like those I am familiar with in the Florida—Alabama Gulf Coast regions. When conversation turns to Australia, I am alert for any reference to Tasmania. Unfortunately, it is seldom mentioned. Kangaroos, "The Outback," Ayers Rock, Sydney, and Melbourne get all the news. Tasmania remains an undiscovered paradise.

In that respect, the Northwest Florida paradise has been something of an equal. The only time our piece of geography

179

is mentioned in the national news is when there is a hurricane of massive proportions bearing down on it. (Too bad that in 1561 Tristan de Luna didn't have a color TV set with a 24-hour weather channel.)

Lloyd attended trade schools and learned welding. He learned to scuba dive. He worked for a time near Alice Springs, building and repairing giant trucks to haul mineral ore. He served in the Australian Army. He became a "jack of all trades." More recently, he became a partner in a fishing enterprise.

He and the Skipper, his partner, sail the "Wild Wind," a two-masted fishing schooner, in search of sharks, lobster, and other commercially valuable sea life. When he isn't fishing, he is welding.

A couple of years ago, Lloyd and the Skipper took time off to sail up the eastern side of the continent of Oceania. They visited twenty or more small islands and coral reefs. In the process, they took photographs and kept notes on plant and animal life for the Australian Department of National Parks and Wildlife. With the help of a Parks Officer, they collected samples of the flora and fauna.

There are times as I push a pencil across my desk that I wish Lloyd and I could exchange places for awhile. Somehow, sailing the "Wild Wind" and hunting sharks sounds like the way life was meant to be lived. On the other hand, I expect Lloyd breathes a foggy sigh of despair when he is hauling in a net for the third time in a day. When the cold water freezes his raw hands blue, he must wish he could exchange places with me and my pencil for just a bit of centrally heated time.

Lloyd came to visit us in Atlanta in 1979. A healthy lobster season gave him extra cash to burn. We met for the first time at the Atlanta airport. If either of us spoke English, it was not discernable to the other. Four days of conversation were required for either of us to gain an "ear" for what the other was saying. Karen and I enjoyed Lloyd's visit just as we would a visit from a long-lost relative.

He returned to Tasmania and continues to keep us abreast of life "Down Under." These days, we keep Lloyd informed of life in New Jersey.

I should mention that Lloyd is still single. I wonder if any single women out there would be interested in meeting him? What a date that would be. Travel half way around the world for your date with Lloyd. A candlelight dinner of boiled lobster. Meet the fine citizens of Stanley. Sit on the porch swing and watch the stars. The "Southern Cross" might never be so beautiful! I'll buy dinner for the two of you. All you have to do is get there.

The Commonwealth of Australia celebrated its 200th Anniversary in 1988. I hope Lloyd, his family, and his fellow countrymen had a splendid celebration as they began their third century as a nation.

§§§§§§§

THE LAST OF THE BRITISH EMPIRE

It seemed proper to me that the remnants of the British Empire would meet in Germany. After all, the Royal Family of England is of German descent. Since 1714 the "Merrie Isle" has struck coinage carrying images of the royal family of Hanover—a German family. And you thought the Queen of England was of English blood. Nay! Not since Mary Queen of Scots has this been true. It is enough to make a Scotsman shed a tear.

It was a business meeting. Several English-speaking countries where my company sells its wares were represented. Of course, the American Colonies were there too, represented by me and by three additional patriots.

When the facts are known, it is surprising we Americans speak any English at all. When the Declaration of Independence was signed and sent out for publication by the press, it was a German-language newspaper that first carried the text. It scooped the English-language papers in Philadelphia by more than a day.

At the turn of this century, Congress voted on a resolution to make the German language the official language of the United States. The measure failed by a single vote.

Winston Churchill, when but a foolish lad, was captured in battle and held as a prisoner of war. The country in which that event occurred was also represented at our meeting. The British lost that war too, reducing the size of the Empire by yet another country.

The British colony founded by prisoners (as was Georgia) had a representative there. Of course, that country is no longer a colony either. It's a full-fledged nation with hardy citizens—like "Crocodile Dundee"—inhabiting its lands.

The North American country that can't seem to make up its mind whether its origins are French or English was represented. In the winter you will find half its population in Panama City, Florida, sunning themselves and believing that the weather that time of year is as warm as it gets.

I found it interesting that I could understand the Canadian quite well. I could understand the South African with a little interpretive help from the Germans. I pretended to understand the Australian. Almost everything an Australian says is funny. So, even if I could not understand what was said, I laughed anyway, just to be polite.

Our "Mother Country," Great Britain, was represented at our meeting by four Brits. Each was from a different city in Britain and each spoke a different dialect. Not one word was intelligible to me. We were fortunate to have German interpreters to help us to understand our own Mother Tongue.

"Y'all show do tawk funneh," I said. They laughed out of courtesy and then asked a German to interpret what I had said.

"Repeat after me," I said in an instructive voice. "The rayne en Spuayne fawls muainly own de pulayne." (The rain in Spain falls mainly on the plain.)

One Brit tried his best and said, "The waw-er in Majorca, ain't wot it ort-a." (The water in Majorca is not what it should be if, indeed, most of the rain falls on the plains in Spain.)

George Bernard Shaw once said, "The Americans and the Britons have everything in common except language."

Bubba, like, if that dude ain't right on, like, grits ain't groceries. Y'know what I mean?

$$\oint\oint\oint\oint\oint\oint$$

THE GREASY PIG CONTEST

May Day, 1987. I was in Wiesenheim Am Berg—(Wiesenheim by the mountain) in the Rhine Pfalz area of Germany. It was a holiday for my German colleagues. My friends, the Zeltwangers, entertained me for the day at their home and in their town.

There was a May pole in the village square near the Lutheran Church. The Church rector, Herr Fischer, had arranged for toys to be attached near the top of the May Pole. It was up to the hardiest of the children to climb to the top and remove the toys for themselves and their friends.

Fritz, Sebastian, Susi, Wolfgang, Christa, and Steffi (among others) made an effort. If I'd worn my climbing clothes, I would have tried it myself. Some of the toys were very appealing. There was a soccer ball, a dart board, and a skateboard.

In this village of some 1400 inhabitants, the language of laughter and enjoyment echoed from walls that were built over 800 years ago. One could picture the same festivities taking place amid the same scenery many centuries ago.

I suppose I enjoyed all the amusement so much because it reminded me of the "Fun Night" we had in Chumuckla the fall of 1960. It was then that some enterprising, fun-loving, Ruritan Club member dreamed up the "Greased Pole" contest and the "Greasy-Pig" roundup.

It was a difficult challenge to climb the fifteen-foot greased pole. It was important to wait until the initial challengers had significantly depleted the supply of grease on the pole in their efforts to reach the top. My winning strategy involved rolling myself in dirt and sand and coating my bare belly with grit. My hands were filled with sand, increasing my traction on the pole.

Campbell Salter gave Buddy Robinette a merciful boost to the top. Buddy and I captured five-dollar bills from the top of the Greased Pole. We earned a photo of ourselves in the Press Gazette.

Even with my filthy, grit-laden body, however, I was unable to grasp the "Greasy Pig." The pig was let loose on the football field, where he ran for life amid twenty-five screaming, sweating, dirt-caked adolescents.

I grabbed its greasy leg just once, but the more I squeezed to hold on, the more the pig slipped away. Jimmy had him, then Benny. Next, the pig popped through Neal's arms and into Sally's. The wily pig slipped away from Sally and through eleven other kids before Tommy Richarme captured him with a flying body tackle. Tommy kept the pig.

Somebody should sponsor a "Greasy Pig" roundup again. I would give up Vanna White and the Wheel of Fortune to see one good pig chase. I think I would not want to participate again, however—at least, not if there is a formal dress requirement.

$$\oint\oint\oint\oint\oint\oint\oint$$

EUROPE...AS IT WERE (1985)

I consider myself to be well traveled. I have crossed "Murder Creek" to shop at McGowan's Hardware Store in

Brewton, Alabama. I have seen the Agri-Rama in Tifton, Georgia. I have feasted on fresh fried mullet at Nichols' Seafood Restaurant in Bagdad, Florida. Even so, I revelled in the opportunity to visit Europe with some of my cultured business friends. We came by our culture on the "back forties" of the nation. Most of it clings to our shoes. Our culture is of the "agri" variety.

My company manufactures synthetic vitamins. These I help market to the American Feed Industry. Customers and "corporate junketeers" took advantage of an opportunity to visit the parent company office in Germany to see Europe. Many of us had never been "Over There, Over There."

The group consisted of buyers and sellers of feed ingredients for the commodities of animal agriculture. Feed mills and feed ingredients are familiar. The average chemical plant is foreign to us all.

We toured the massive German chemical production site for the company. It is near Mannheim, a town at the intersection of the Rhine and Neckar Rivers. There, a forest of modern chemical engineering extends for five miles along the banks of the Rhine. Over 50,000 people are employed at the site. A thousand rail cars arrive at and leave  the complex facility every day. Hundreds of trucks and barges make daily exchanges of cargo at the site.

A chemical plant is a "plumber's heaven"; plenty of pipes in this chemical mega-factory. Blue pipes, yellow pipes, green pipes, red pipes, silver pipes; big pipes, little pipes, short pipes, and long pipes. Mostly long pipes and mostly big pipes. It is the largest chemical production site in the world.

We were awed. Before this, a "double-six herringbone" milking parlor ranked Number 1 in pipe complexity—followed closely by a dual-exhaust Chevy pickup. My point of reference was now redefined.

Our German colleagues went an extra kilometer to present their country in a first-class way. Boat down the Rhine. Stone castles every quarter of a mile. The ruins spoke to us of another era and time-forgotten marauders.

The castles were much larger than the average Alabama Chateau. The style and beauty of medieval architecture demanded appreciation. Oh! What those people could have done in days of old if only they had access to styrofoam, chrome-plated plastic, virgin vinyl, and super glue.

Fine foods! Savory East Bay Oysters served on the half shell, circa 1965, came to mind for me. But now there is a new memory.

After a memorable dinner in the town of Weyher at an inn overlooking lush, manicured vineyards, Jerry Westphal of "Golden Sun Feeds" remarked wistfully that Bud's Cafe in Esterville, Iowa, would never again hold quite the same reverent place in his heart.

At Worms there is a large cathedral. Martin Luther defended his case for the "Protestant Movement" there—history. A change of course.

Antique medieval instruments made music as we dined at "The Golden Fleece" in the historic town of Heidelberg. Revelry.Next came Rudesheim. More revelry. Dancing in the streets with a German ladies bowling league in town to celebrate a victory.

Next day: Paris. Beyond my expectations—Paris, it seems, must be touched to be believed. Monumental monuments. Historic history. A builder's paradise of architecture and—the food.

Think Paris. Think—wrought iron filigree on every building. The city is a living antique. In America, *old is 1910, 1830—maybe even 1560.*

In Paris, "recent" is when they laid the cornerstone for "Le Cathedrale Notre Dame." That was about 300 years before the Italian chap rented some Spanish ships in 1492, set out for China, and ran afoul of a whole bunch of naked savages in "die neue wert."

Boat ride on the Seine. More good food. A show. There was much to "show" at the show. This was the Paris that demanded to be seen. And it was. It was real "art." At least, that is what I keep telling my wife.

Someday, I hope to visit North Dakota (the reason escapes me at the moment). In my travels, I want to tour "Beauvoir," the home of Jefferson Davis in Biloxi, Mississippi.

Somehow, though, I feel even these gems of tourism will not measure up to the European junket. Europe will be in my future travels and the next time—my wife insists on joining me.

$$\phi\phi\phi\phi\phi\phi\phi$$

AN INTERNATIONAL INCIDENT NARROWLY AVOIDED

With a name like Campbell and a Scottish heritage, you might expect me to take advantage of a free trip to Germany.

It is a business trip. It is May. I am in Mannheim, a young German city—most of it under 200 years old. Much is rebuilt since the last war.

I enjoy, alone, an outdoor cafe called "Der Goldner Adler" (Golden Eagle). I sip a glass of cold German *milk*; watch the people.

A grandmother with purple hair passes me by. She looks at me as if I am from outer space—must be my gaping mouth.

The town drunk salutes the ladies as they pass by on parade. A dog (German Shepherd, of course) chases a frisbee across the cobblestone courtyard.

A talented fellow begins playing a bagpipe in the middle of the square. The music is haunting. It echoes from the surrounding buildings. This German chap must have captured the bagpipe on a hunting trip in Scotland. I am told these many-legged creatures are abundant in the hills there.

Leaving my restful location, I wander to the River Neckar and walk upstream—observe the city and the boat traffic. Darkness approaches.

In broken German, I ask a lady whether the railroad track nearby will bring a streetcar to get me back to my hotel. In broken English, she tells me it will.

A young fellow nearby overhears the English conversation. He asks me whether I am American. He looks displeased. I take a risk and tell him, "Yes...I am American."

He angrily says something in German. "Ichgarowzigunduspatingamilaudensigsenzaphelgritlesgrundinuclear. U.S.A., begitzenspinlegramergitchenhefflingobber." I think that's what he said, and it sounded like bad news for an American.

For just such an incident, I had with me in my back pocket a folded up sign that says "Yankee Go Home." I figured it's better to join 'em than to fight 'em.

But before I took this precaution, I asked the fellow, "Bitte, was ist das auf English, Bubba?" (What does that mean in English, Bubba?)

He said, "Your NHL (National Hockey League) did not support the German league in its dispute with the Finnish league. This has upset the German hockey fans, especially since we won the dispute in court anyway. Your NHL should be ashamed."

It is with a great sigh of relief that I reply, "I agree. I'll speak with the President about the issue as soon as I return." An international incident was avoided. I boarded the streetcar and traveled to my hotel.

§§§§§§§

A LASTING MEMENTO

We wanted to share our European trip with our nieces and nephews. The challenge would be to bring them some special memento—something instructive for the little people.

We gave it serious thought.

Would Kevin like a plastic cuckoo clock from Germany? Would Mary Beth enjoy having a genuine plastic replica of the Eiffel Tower (made in Taiwan)? And Jason, surely he would like to have a detailed replica of a Napoleonic cannon with molded plastic cannoneers, all made to 1/100 scale and imported from the Minnesota Collectors Mint in Lake Woebetide, Minnesota.

For Anna Ruth, perhaps a pink plastic castle made in Haiti and assembled in the United Kingdom. A set of plastic knights might spark Christopher's imagination. And Benjamin might like a pair of vinyl "lederhosen," an imitation of the leather pants worn by Bavarians who want to impress tourists.

Tamara will want a bottle of French perfume. But with the current exchange rate, it might be cheaper to sell our Oldsmobile to raise enough cash to buy a bottle in the United States.

What would Wesley want? What, we thought? Who knows?

We asked Grandma Gatewood for ideas. She was a school teacher for many years. Maybe she would have some ideas on what to bring these imaginative youngsters.

She could think of no trinkets that might satisfy, but mentioned that she had brought rocks back from her Grand Canyon trip. Her Grandsons, Jason and Christopher, had enjoyed them beyond belief. They take them out and show them to visitors and say, "Now this rock here is from the Grand Canyon, and this one is from...."

"Voila!" we said. Our problem is solved. We would bring back a rock from each country we visited, one for each nephew and niece. They couldn't break them easily. They would last forever. And they would be genuine souvenirs—not plastic reproductions.

Once we started looking for rocks, it became great fun for us. In Germany, I would point out a picturesque view of a castle, and Karen would say, "Just a minute, I've found a rock.

In France, Karen was awed by the Eiffel Tower lit up at night. Excitedly she said, "Look! Look, Vic! It's beautiful. It looks like spun gold!"

"I'll be along in a minute. There are some fantastic rocks here on the pathway!" I responded.

The same thing happened at Napoleon's Tomb and the Arc de Triomphe.

Who knows whose head might have rolled over those rocks during the French Revolution? King Louis? Marie Antionette? We were walking all over history.

We may have missed a few tourist sights, but we came home with a suitcase full of great rocks.

$$\oint\oint\oint\oint\oint\oint\oint$$

JUNIOR GOES TO WASHINGTON

Junior Wade, a fellow classmate from Chumuckla School—and a perpetual teenager—visited Washington D.C. for the first time recently. He was there to attend a salesmen's convention for his company. His wife, Brenda, who teaches history at King Middle School, was allowed to join him on the trip. It's a good thing, because she might have committed spouse-icide if she had not. Murder, you understand, is a *"CapitOl"* offense.

Karen and I joined them. It is only a short drive to Washington D.C. from New Jersey. And I wanted to see for myself whether Junior could get the government straightened out. He has political ambitions. If the office of "County Line" ever opens up, he may run for it.

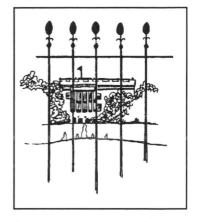

Since we had been to the Capitol before, we acted as tour guides. We showed them where the restrooms were in The American Museum of Natural History. We showed them how to buy soft drinks from street vendors to avoid dehydration. We showed them how to pay fifteen dollars for a ten-minute horse carriage tour around a city block. The main point of interest on this tour was how the buildings are put together with no mortar between the stone blocks. Can't buy too much in Washington, D.C. for fifteen dollars.

We pointed out some tall monuments—and some short ones. We took pictures of big buildings and some little ones. We drove around in heavy traffic, circling the same monument six times until we figured out the correct way to turn, which is the opposite direction one would expect. If you think about it, Washington never turns the way one would expect. As a matter of fact, that is one of the things that brings America the respect of its enemies. They never know what "Those Crazy Americans" are going to do next. Even we Americans have no idea what we will do next.

We saw The Declaration of Independence, The Constitution of The United States of America, and The Bill Of Rights. "Liberty and Justice for All," they said.

To increase their vacation excitement level, Junior planned to jump off the top of the Washington Monument with a hang glider. Fortunately for Brenda and their kids, we found other excitement. We caught a Russian taking pictures of The White House.

After vowing among ourselves not to give away any military secrets, especially not the location of the National Guard Armory down home, we invited the Russian to join us for dinner. It was a ploy. Covertly, we wanted to learn more about these Russians.

O.K. So she wasn't a spy. So the Russian was a lady in her sixties—a Russian immigrant and naturalized American, who came to this country from Germany in the early 1950s. She could have been a spy, but she wasn't. At least I don't believe she was.

Marina Dubrowin (doo-brrov-nin, roll the "r") recently retired from her work at the United Nations in New York, where she continues to live. She was on vacation, just as we were, to rekindle her awe in this Republic we call the United States.

We met her when she asked us to take her picture in front of the White House. Junior Brenda, and the two of us took advantage of this chance meeting. We asked the lady to join us for dinner.

The history lesson was unadulterated—direct from a participant. That is the way I most enjoy history. In her lifetime, this woman has seen the greatest of changes. Her father was a colonel in the engineering corps of the Czarist Army (the White Russians). You may have seen them briefly in the movie, "Dr. Zhivago." They lost, by the way, to the Bolsheviks (Red Russians).

She and her family lived in Western Siberia for years. Then they lived in Southern Russia. They survived the "Stalinist Purge," but were displaced to Germany when the Nazi army invaded Russia. They were fortunate to have some German relatives to ease somewhat the extremes of a wartime labor camp. There, they lived and worked, under American and British bombs, until the end of World War II.

After the war, she emigrated to America and worked in Washington for a time as a translator. Later, she found a job at the United Nations.

Brenda, who teaches history, understood much more than the rest of us. We tried to correct Mrs. Dubrowin's pronunciation several times. We had learned the names of the rivers and mountains of Russia from experts. Our high school teachers, Cal Bodenstein, and The Reverend Hunsucker, certainly pronounced "Dnieper River" correctly. She *insisted*, however, that her pronunciation was correct. Stubborn, these Russians.

We learned of "The Time of Troubles" in the late 1500s, when the boy Prince, Dmitri, expired, leaving no male heir to the throne. Another chap claimed to be Dmitri. Some years later, this "False Dmitri" rounded up a Polish army and took over Moscow. He ruled for a few years, until death by *accurate* puncture. Then came more invaders, and then came the Romanovs. The Romanovs were still in power when our dinner guest was born.

She told us about Anton Chekhov, a famous Russian, who in no way is associated with the "Star Trek" television series. Apparently, he was the Russian equivalent of William "What Light Through Yonder Window Breaks?" Shakespeare.

Marina told us about the "boy hero" Paulik Morozov (Paul Frost), who told on his parents when they clung to "capitalist ideals." His parents were banished to prison. There was a statue built to honor the boy. Children were encouraged to inform the "party officials" when their parents were less-than-ideal communists.

Marina expressed the hope that some of the disruptive practices of the Soviet system in the past are toning down now. She explained how Nikita "The Shoe Pounder" Khrushchev had tried to de-Stalinize the Soviet system in the 1960s and institute some reforms. He was not a politician though. The Politburo bounced him out of office and put him back on the farm.

We told Marina that Khrushchev put the scare on Florida when he tried missile reform in Cuba. I, for one, dug a hole four feet deep in the woods behind our house. I covered it with a piece of tin from the hog barn. With my bunker prepared, I was ready for nuclear war. I stocked my bomb shelter with some of my best marbles and a few "Richie Rich" and "Archie" comic books. I took my BB gun and waited two solid hours one day for the attack. When it started to rain, the bunker flooded and became cold, oozing red clay. I quit the war at that point and left it to the professionals.

We had come to Washington to learn more about America, and in the process, we learned a great deal about Russia. The USSR, explained our guest, ruled not only over Russia, but over Latvia, Estonia, Kazakhstan, and eleven other "states" as well.

In a way though, you could say our history lesson on Russia gave us a much greater appreciation of the country whose Capitol we had come to visit.

"In Order To Form A More Perfect Union...."

I hope Junior's kids will not tell on him for talking to a Russian. At least, he didn't jump off the Washington Monument in a hang glider.

§§§§§§§

VIII

The Bureaucracy of Business

"We trained hard—but it seemed that
every time we were beginning to form up into teams
we would be reorganized....
I was to learn later in life
that we tend to meet any new situation by reorganizing;
and a wonderful method it can be
for creating the illusion of progress
while producing confusion, inefficiency and demoralization."

Petronius: 210 B.C.

CORN PLANTING—THE CORPORATE WAY

For two solid weeks, I have been helping my boss prepare a business proposal for upper management. Before the VP presents the proposal to the Chairman of the Board, however, the President wants to review our thinking. He requires a "pre-presentation."

"Take this part out," says he. "Put this part in."

Before the President sees it, though, we have a request from our overseas trading partners to see a preview of what it is the President will look at (a sort of "pre-pre-presentation").

"Don't say this," they say with a foreign accent. "Say that. We don't want to tell them too much!"

The Business Director will be out of the country at the time, so he needs a "pre-pre-pre-presentation."

"You crazy, or what!" he exclaims. "You have to tell every detail; leave nothing out."

When "Mr. Big" finally sees the proposal, it will be presented and over within less than 15 minutes. For two rigorous weeks, we've been writing and editing and rewriting. We practiced presentations. We drew graphs with a computer plotter.

From all appearances, you'd think nobody trusts anybody to make the proper presentation to the Chairman.

Farming seemed so much easier. No bureaucracy to respond to. Only the fates of nature. Make your choices and take your chances.

Pop said, "Take this seed corn and this hoe and plant that ten-acre field."

I did it. That was that. No checking and double-checking to confirm the decision.

After six acres, I was tired. After eight acres, I was exhausted. I dumped the remainder of my seed corn in a shallow hole and covered it with moist, brown earth. "There. All done. Quitting time!"

Who would know?

Later in the Spring, as Pop cultivated the corn, he chanced upon a dense growth of young corn plants at the end of the last row. The evidence was incriminating.

We had a smaller corn crop than Pop intended that year. From that time on, Pop was more strict in his supervision. He double-checked everything I did.

I wonder whether somebody told our company President about the corn?

Anyway, I hope the result of our well-prepared presentation is the Chairman's approval of a new coffee maker for our department.

THE O—N SWITCH MAKES ALL THE DIFFERENCE

In the office where I work, there is a computer. It is of the personal variety. The I.B.A. Wizard Company took great care to create a machine that humanoids could understand. Unfortunately, there are times when the collective brain power of individuals in my department is insufficiently programmed to manage the beastly box of chips.

Only last week, we were unable to turn it on.

My assistant, Sasche, a veritable genius with the computer, informed me that the main power switch failed to start the machine. The printer cranked up. The monitor cranked up. But the computer just sat there; no life, no computation, no friendly message. Just silence.

"Call the I.B.A. Wizard help desk," I suggested. "Surely, they will have an explanation."

Sasche phoned the androids that know all the controls and all the answers for malfunctioning computers of the I.B.A. Wizard variety.

"Ms. G. Wizz speaking."

"G. Wizz, this is Sasche. My computer will not come on when I turn on the main switch. What could be wrong?"

"Well", said Ms. Wizz, "The internal laser doppler interface may be out of sync. If that's not the problem, you might check the core memory nuclear mnemonic device located beneath the interlocular post-mandibular RGB connection. In any case, the estimated cost of repair is $4,792.17."

"Oh," she replied.

After Sasche informed me of the discussion with the I.B.A. Wizard help desk, I suggested that she find another computer user in the building and look for a less-expensive solution. I stayed with the wounded machine, hoping the problem might only be a blown fuse.

Fred, who delivers our office mail, stopped by to console me for a moment.

"What's the problem?" Fred asked.

"Computer's broken."

"Mind if I look?"

"Go ahead, can't hurt."

Fred fiddled with it a second, and the thing came to life. A friendly message appeared on the monitor and the internal disc began to hum.

"What did you do, Fred?"

"Well," he said, "you had the power on at the main switch, but the *Owen switch* on the computer was in the *Owe eph eph* position." And he walked off, whistling a few bars of music from Rossini's "William Tell Overture". An image of the "Lone Ranger" flashed briefly through my cerebral cortex.

I stared blankly at the computer.

"The 'Owen Switch'?" I said. "The *Owen Switch?*" I said again. "I wonder what that is? Sasche better call the help desk and get a definition for it. It sounds incredibly simple, but the meaning escapes me."

§§§§§§§

THE PINK ZONE

Irascible, infuriating, irritating, insufferable. Adjectives which, when used in conjunction with one another, describe the anthropoidal species known in business as a National Sales Manager. They were created by God to provide a natural enemy to Product Managers in their quest for success.

I am a Product Manager, a marketing-type techno-humanoid being. A National Sales Manager for my company, Mel Hoyt is a survivor of WWII "Kamikazi" attacks, endless conventions in nameless towns, the administrations of many presidents from the "wrong" party, and the stock market crashes of 1929 and 1987. He is a paragon of persistence.

He can also sell any product I cannot keep in stock, manufacture, or import. He can cut a price faster than you can say "Melvin, it costs more than that to make the stuff!"

Mel is also a native of New York City, known as Gotham, Metropolis, Megalopolis, or—as preferred by some of us enamored with cartography—"The Pink Zone" (note the pink shaded portion of your New York State map).

I am a native of Santa Rosa County, Florida, and we had no "pink zones." Driving a car in Milton was, in another time, a challenge for me. I graduated to the suburbs of Atlanta after many years. But to drive in "I Heart NYC" is an experience that leaves my "karma" in a hopeless state of discombobulation.

Because of this psychic phobia, I chose to ride with Mel across town (through Manhattan), from one business meeting to another. He was the expert.

I tried to keep track of our progress for future reference. Turn left at the tall building and go two blocks. Take a right at the really tall building and, after passing a hot dog stand, take another right at a really, really, really, ta-a-a-l-l-l building. I soon gave up. It must take decades to learn the streets in "I Heart NYC."

It was on Madison Avenue (yes, *The* Madison Avenue) that trouble began. Mel failed to notice a sign that said, "The two right lanes are for the express use of City Buses between the hours of 5:30 p.m. and 7:00 p.m. on odd numbered dates for nine days following the third quarter of the moon and for three months following Yom Kippur." I don't know *how* he missed it.

One of New York's finest stopped us. Mel tried to explain, but soon accepted his fate and waited in the bus lane, while the policeman took his license and car registration. The officer left to fill out the forms. While the first officer was away, a second policeman came to the car and began to write out a ticket for stopping in the bus lane.

It was about that point that an evil smile crept over my lips and a twinkle flashed fiercely from the pupil of my left eyeball.

"Hey! Officer" I said. "This is just like 'Hill Street Blues.' Do you know 'Dog Breath?'(the undercover agent on the TV show). Say, ain't you one of them 'pigs' Mel talks about all the time? Mel wonders if it's true yo' momma would squeal if we pulled her tail? Hey Mel, ain't this fun. I never had so much fun in Noo Yawk befow!"

The officer was not happy. My evil plan was working better than I had dreamed.

Soon Mel had a *second* traffic ticket that would send him to prison for the rest of his natural irritability.

Sometimes it is fun to be a Product Manager.

§§§§§§§

BATTLECAR BUREAUCRATICA

My first officer is Dr. Charlie Yacomeni. Charlie is a Scotsman. His accent tempts me to call him "Scotty," but the dangers ahead of us caution me not to anger him. I will need a friend in this unfriendly place.

Charlie is not a "Real Doctor (the *medical* kind)." He holds no "R.D." degree. He is a doctor of philosophy—a PhD chemist. His degree was conferred by the University of Edinburgh, Scotland. The school is not accredited by Florida, Georgia, or Alabama. It is good, however, that he is a chemist, because chemists are generally well armed with epithets and expletives. We will need a full complement of these weapons this morning.

We strap ourselves in the cockpit. We bring the machine about. I call for power: rpm's. The machine acknowledges that it will perform. The rpm's increase as I edge the thrusters forward even more; and we enter a steady course, predetermined by High Command only the day before.

We are passed on the port side by a low profile sleek machine, piloted by a young, blonde, female captain—probably a member of the youth brigade. Their machines are surely subsidized by their genetic donors. The incident appears to create no problem for us. We log the occurrence (Stardate 1987) and continue on our course.

"Red Octagon! Red Octagon! Slow thrusters. Impede forward motion! Bring the machine to a standstill."

"Forward motion has ceased sir," reports the First Officer. "We were almost overcome by the omnipresent inertia, but you have succeeded."

The way is soon clear. We proceed.

"Starboard here, Captain," the First Officer intones. "You forget this pathway every time. You're lucky to have me aboard."

I hate it when he gloats. I bring the machine about, turning ninety degrees to starboard.

We begin to spot bogies on the pathway. It is imperative that we maintain an appearance of "status quo," while the First Officer brings his weapons to the ready. If we are attacked, we must act immediately or risk nonentity.

"Watch that cargo transport, Charlie," I say, forgetting formalities. "He's bearing down on us! Fire! Fire!"

Officer Yacomeni is already prepared. He fires one epithet, then another. A single photon gesture saves us. Though shaken, our ego is intact.

Soon we begin to enter a large spaceway with numerous contacts. The enemy is visible as far as the eye can see. We are surrounded. It will take all of our skill to overcome the hostile intentions of the hordes. I order shields in place. At 0700 hours the solar glare on this planet can generate a blinding experience. We enter the vortex.

We execute a daring maneuver to port and force two bogies to stall as we enter the attack pattern from the starboard side. They fire a barrage of expletives and four photon gestures. But we are saved as Charlie fires a quick burst of multiple epithets.

For good measure, Charlie throws a perfectly executed facial contortion from our after-view device. The two bogies are crippled and thoroughly enraged. We force yet another confrontation as we speed forward—rpm's high and gear ratio low.

At last, we merge into freeway traffic—only a brief battle before us until we exit to the safety of Bureaucratica, the Super Nauseam—"The Office."

Charlie and I carpool regularly to the office. Where we work, in the national headquarters for a multi-galactic chemical concern, our work is more than just a job—*it's an adventure.*

[For those who are not Trekkies, we offer the following translations: Machine = car; red octagon = stop sign; genetic donor = parent; bogey = enemy contact (car); cargo transport = eighteen wheeler.]

§§§§§§

PAID TO TRAVEL

Shortly after I began my education at Pensacola Junior College, I ran out of money. I sold my last cow and did not have time to pick butterbeans and peas for my cousin, T. D. Salter. Jobs were not easy to come by. I was fortunate to land one with the educational TV station on campus, Station WSRE-TV. They made me an assistant to the photographer, and there I stayed until I left the junior college for the University of West Florida.

I was lucky. Tim Burch, who was president of our high school class (17 people), was even more in need of money than I was. He too, had no time to pick cotton, or peas, or okra. Besides, cotton-picking machines were in vogue by then, and they had put a lot of cotton pickers out of business.

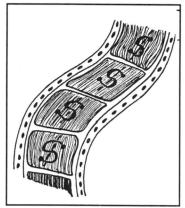

Tim was one of the first people I knew to discover there were things called "positions." It seems that there are some people who have "jobs" and some people who have "positions." Tim fell into a deal at the educational TV station that accurately fit the description of "position," instead of "job." The TV station paid Tim to watch movies. He would review all of the 16-millimeter documentary films and travelogues that came to the station for broadcast. He had to check to be sure they were suitable and that they would not break in the middle of a show.

Tim sat in a dark room for hours, watching movies about exotic places all over the world. It was an eye opener. The experience itself was an education.

Today, Tim has a "position" with a pharmaceutical firm. He represents his company in Alabama and lives near Birmingham. He now has an opportunity to travel to some of the places he used to see in the movies.

As for me, after jobs picking okra, clearing new ground, planting corn, and picking cotton, the desire to find a salaried "position" became very strong. My quest for a suitable one has taken me from the Gulf of Tonkin to Ludwigshafen, Germany, and even to foreign places like New Jersey.

After many years, I thought I had found a "position." I thought I had *arrived*. (Inside work, no heavy lifting.) Last week reality took its inevitable course. My boss reviewed my annual performance.

He praised my 12-hour days, my team spirit, my computer expertise, and my market surveys. I felt a fair measure of pride. Then he said, "But, you know, Vic, you can do a better "job." This "job" demands a lot. There is a lot of "work" to be done around here." On and on he went about "The Job." Oh well, at least, it beats picking okra.

ƒƒƒƒƒƒƒ

EAT MORE BEEF

The price of beef is going up and up. The price of poultry products is dropping. Have you ever wondered why these things go in cycles? I have, and I have done an extensive study on the phenomenon involved.

Only a couple of years ago, there seemed to be no end to the demand for chicken. Nobody could get enough. Claims of low cholesterol and high protein were gospel. At the time, I was working closely with the beef industry, and the poor cattlemen were at a loss—not knowing how to counter the chicken threat.

I had some bumper stickers made up that said "Support Beef, Run Over a Chicken." I gave them to cattlemen all over the Southeast. Dorothy and John Creel, of Allentown, took a number of them to give to customers of their feed store. Cattlemen sincerely felt threatened by the "feathered menace."

Within months, in an odd turn of events, I was working in a new job in the poultry industry. I had to get rid of my bumper stickers. The poultry industry is big corporate business. I couldn't afford to drive up to a corporate poultry office loudly proclaiming "death to the chicken" on my front bumper.

Then two things happened. First, 60 Minutes (the TV show) ran an exposé on poultry processing and the sanitary conditions in some of the plants. Reports of bacterial contamination in poultry products followed. More recently, there have been reports of contaminated eggs.

These problems are ever present. Government and Industry groups are constantly working to improve the quality of food sold to the American consumers. But the public is rarely given a hard look at the real problems in food preparation on a massive scale.

The second thing that happened was that on October 14, 1986 at 8:30 p.m. (Pacific Time), a well-dressed urban yuppie who was dining in a well-known Northern California "Nouvelle Cuisine" restaurant, in front of several other restaurant patrons—and with no remorse in his voice—said rather loudly, "Please take this stupid two-ounce, broiled-in-olive-oil, bland, unfilling (but well-presented) dish of chicken breast and bring me a fourteen-ounce, medium-rare Cajun Steak, fit for a man and his dog."

The rest is history.

Within weeks there were restaurants all over America serving Cajun steaks, Cajun catfish with broiled beef (Pond and Pasture), and Cajun pizza with cubed steak toppings. Cajun steaks were served coast to coast. As soon as the government program to make hamburger out of dairy cows was over, the price of beef began to move upward.

For the cattlemen who survived the long, unprofitable years of not so long ago, there is now sweet music in the sound of the auctioneer's voice in livestock sale barns all over the nation.

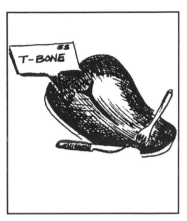

I still enjoy chicken, and I savor the tast of well-prepared fish. Beef, however, remains one of my very favorite dishes.

§§§§§§§

BUY LOW, SELL HIGH

It is supposed to be easy to make money in the stock market. I am told, all you have to do is "Buy Low, and Sell High."

Before the big "crash" of the late '80s, I was told all you had to do was "Buy high and sell even higher." After the crash, I was told all you had to do was "Sell low, and buy even lower."

Well, it has all been an educational experience. An MBA from Harvard might have been cheaper, but I don't know whether it would have been as impressive. A better education might have been to study the Jay Livestock Market a little more carefully before I tried to play "The Big Board."

The only problem I have with studying the Jay Livestock Market is that the professor is a little difficult to understand.

"Gimmefow, fownahalf, five, five, five, whoogimme six?" says the man who spits into the microphone. "Ungala simmee see mo beef ona hoof and a dolla too nine dee nine, SOWED TOO DA MAN INDA BACK BY DERWINDER."

The poor man was only trying to scratch his nose, and he bought a Holstein bull only weeks from hamburger heaven.

The price of beef goes up. The price of beef goes down. Hogs are selling cheap, and then you'll pay any price for a sow and six pigs. One year, goats will be in; weekend farmers need them to keep the briars down. The next year they are out.

If you have ever wondered where burgers come from, or if you know already but just miss the flavor of another era, you should visit the Jay Livestock Sale Barn. Watch the sale. Observe the farmers as they comment to one another on the quality of this or that animal.

If you can understand the man who wears the cowboy hat, chews tobacco, and assaults the microphone with strange syllables, you may be well on your way to understanding the livestock market. From there, it is a small step for an investor to dance into the "other-stock" market.

Just remember, it is very easy to make a small fortune in the "other-stock" market. But you need to start out with a large fortune. And never, never,

never forget to "Buy High and Sell Low"—or is it the other way around?

$$\oint\oint\oint\oint\oint\oint\oint$$

OLD COTTON PICKERS NEVER DIE—THEY JUST TRANSFER TO ANOTHER STATE

I met Lorenzo Howard in New Jersey, at my company's national headquarters. He is the Group Human Resources Manager for the division I work in (when I work)

He tells me he developed a large part of his philosophy toward working with people in the years that he was a cotton picker. He observed the parental qualities of his father, James "Son" Howard, of Pollard, Alabama, and the management style of Frank Smith, of Jay, Florida.

In the years between 1956 and 1966, Lorenzo was a young man who learned the value of work in cotton fields owned by the Smith family. He also learned from Mr. Smith's style of leadership. Treat people as individuals. Treat people with fairness. Treat people with a genuine attitude of concern for their best interests.

Mr. Smith drove a truck to Brewton, Pollard, and Flomanton, Alabama, where young workers joined him for a trip to the cotton fields.

The cotton pickers included Mrs. Georgia Square (and her family) from Flomanton. Raymond and Theodore Walton, Bobby and Johnny Miller, Melvin Howard (Lorenzo's brother), and Charles McGill were among the mostly youthful crew.

According to Lorenzo, Mrs. Square could pick between three- and four-hundred pounds of cotton in a single day.

One major learning experience for Lorenzo and the others occurred when the boys played too rough one day, and one boy was injured. Mr. Smith punished the boys by paying all their day's wages to the injured boy, who was not able to work for several days. It was a good lesson.

Lorenzo's earnings helped to pay for his education at at one of the first accredited, private, black high schools in Alabama, "Southern Normal School." He thinks it is interesting that he is a Baptist who attended schools supported by the Reform Church of North America. (His Bachelor's Degree is from Hope College in Michigan). These were black schools. Later, he attended Aquinas College for his Master's Degree. That school is a Catholic college (98 percent white). Now, he lives in New Jersey and works with a German chemical company. It could be said that Lorenzo is adaptable.

After college Lorenzo taught school. He joined a chemical company as a laboratory technician. He advanced steadily to Research Technician, Production Supervisor, Quality Control Supervisor, and then Manager of Training and Development. Now he is a Group Manager of Human Resources at the company where I work. Not bad for a former cotton picker.

"Son" Howard died some years ago. Lorenzo's mother still lives in Pollard. Charles McGill became a school teacher in Thomasville, Alabama. Melvin Howard and Raymond Walton live and work in Flomanton. Lorenzo last heard from Bobby Miller in Sharon, Pennsylvania, and he heard that Johnny Miller attended Penn State University, but has lost track of him.

Theodore Walton survived Vietnam, but finally succumbed to the effects of Agent Orange.

These cotton pickers have built a legacy. I, too, picked cotton in those years. There is a special respect among old cotton pickers for one another. Lorenzo certainly has mine.

One day soon, we plan to get a jug of ice water and sit down together at my house in New Jersey. We will turn on a heat lamp and pretend we are in Santa Rosa County at the end of the longest row of cotton ever planted. We will perspire under the burning lamp and talk of days that are no more and probably never will be again. And we will be glad that there was a special crop of people in that time and place. But the ice water will probably never be quite as sweet as it was then.

§§§§§§§

IX

Tis the Season

"There is the gift and there is the giver, and the giver of the gift is the recipient of the greatest gain. This is the law of giving and getting. It is contrary to the normal laws of math and physics."

GETTING CLOSE TO ST. NICK

Before there was a Santa Claus, there was a Rusty Grundin. All around the county, school principals and teachers would ask the question—"Is there really a Rusty Grundin?" Every year, just before schools let out for the Christmas holidays, Mr. Grundin visited every county school. He came disguised as Santa Claus and gave  out gifts to all the children. Sometimes they were "exchange" gifts, and sometimes they were modest Christmas presents collected by the Milton Fire Department. Mr. Grundin was the Fire Chief.

He was Santa Claus for Santa Rosa County school kids for nearly forty years—maybe even longer. Today, Rusty Grundin is pleasantly retired, living in Milton amid a houseful of memorabilia spanning a life full of good memories.

A few months ago, I tried to find some information for this book. Somebody suggested that I talk to Mr. Grundin. I gave him a call one night about 8 o'clock. He insisted I meet him that night at his house and get the stuff I needed. We met. We talked. At 11:30 p.m., to prove Rusty still has sway among the city's finest, we raided the City Police Department. We used their photocopy machine to duplicate some of the documents he wanted me to have. By the next afternoon, I was back in New Jersey, befuddled and bogged down in corporate bureaucracy, the book falling somewhat lower in priority behind my company paycheck. But the information Mr. Grundin gave me will be invaluable.

While looking at Mr. Grundin's personal museum, he made particular note of one of his special items. He has one of the bricks from a building destroyed in The Great Chicago Fire of 1871. The fire started when Mrs. Patrick O'Leary's cow, surprised by cold hands on a warm udder, kicked over a lantern in the barn. The old bricks are a real collector's item.

Jerry Harris of Chumuckla recently completed brick work for a new home in Milton using bricks recovered from The Great Fire. Jerry is a contractor—one of the esteemed Harris clan known for their superb masonry. Jerry kept some of the bricks. One with a finger print pressed in its side is his favorite. In a way, it defines a kinship between the mason of 1980 and the brick worker of the mid-19th century. The home was built for Bob Murphy; Bob owns a real estate company in Milton.

Can you imagine a whole house finished off with bricks from the famous fire? Rusty Grundin, ex-Fire Chief finds the concept awe inspiring and courageous. Rusty says he is under the impression, though, that the house meets all current building codes for fire prevention and fire safety.

Those of you who enjoy reminiscing would appreciate a visit with Mr. Grundin. You should get in touch with him. What is really needed is somebody to help the old codger get his collection into an organized and genuine museum. It would be an asset to the county.

A visit with the Jolly Old Man may be as close to Santa Claus as you'll ever get.

Yes, Virginia, there is a Rusty Grundin.

A LITTLE WARMTH

He gave his granddaughter, Katherine, enough change to buy a box of King Edward Invincible Deluxe cigars. They would cost thirty-five cents, plus tax. Katherine skipped merrily off to the corner store to buy them, whistling "Jingle Bells" as she went.

"Bo" slipped into memories of years gone by—of France, during "The Great War To End All Wars." He thought of the trenches and the smell of death.

The big guns thundered. The ground shook. The rains fell. The mud deepened. In the trenches, the soldiers experienced a filthy, cold hell.

He remembered how a cigar or a cigarette might become a soldier's only friend and link to a sane world. In those times, smoking was not looked upon as a health hazard. Even if it had been, the risk of a cigarette would be laughable, compared with the front lines of war.

A cigarette was a deodorant and fumigant, to mask the omnipresent, sicky-sweet smell of death.

It became a warm friend, with burning embers that, with imagination, could transport freezing fingers from those cold trenches to a pleasant family hearth.

It was an excuse to light up a match, or a government-issue lighter, for the bright glow of a genuine flame. A soldier could imagine toasting his damp feet by a great roaring fire, first cousin to the flame he held for a brief moment.

A cigarette could be a threatening weapon, warding off rats who shared their new-found homes with the soldiers—both living and dead.

Cigarettes were a kind punctuation mark in an otherwise despairing death sentence on the front lines of battle.

As he dreamed, Uncle Bo remembered a visitor to his part of hell. He had told the story to his wife, Irene, and his daughter, Bernadine, many times.

The visitor approached Bo's shelter of a trench. Bo shivered a challenge, "Who goes there?"

"A friend," piped an old man's voice, as the white-haired fellow spilled from a belly crawl into the pit that was "Bo's" home.

"What's an old man like you doing here?" asked a startled "Bo."

"Here, have a cigarette, soldier," the old fellow said. The gesture spoke volumes. It told him:

- Even when you are in the trenches of life, somebody "out there" cares.

- Somebody, somewhere, remembers you personally.

- With wars on and death all around, kindness can still be found among the living.

- It takes little to warm the heart of he who has nothing.

"What's that strange uniform you're wearing?" asked "Bo," as the little old man clambered out of the pit and crawled to the next.

"Salvation Army," was the fading reply.

Katherine returned from the store. The door slammed behind her and brought grandfather "Bo" back to the present. Tears glistened in Katherine's eyes.

"Grandpa," she said, "I saw an old man ringing a bell and collecting money for the poor outside of the store. I was so sad for them, I gave them your money. I am so sorry. It was wrong for me to do that."

"No child. You did no wrong. Come. Sit with me by this warm and glorious fire and let me tell you a story."

My Great Uncle "Bo," B. O. Langham, died in 1972. He held a special place in his heart for the Salvation Army— and for children.

§§§§§§§

A CHRISTMAS CARD FROM TAIWAN

My hometown is small, but the people there have connections all over the world. No matter where you go on this planet, there is somebody from home who knows somebody or knows somebody who knows somebody in the area you might visit.

The fact was brought home to me in the fall of 1972, when I was in the Navy and my ship was pointed toward the China Sea. While most of the fellows (many of them from much larger towns than I) were making preparations for a "libationary" liberty in the city of Kaohsiung, Taiwan, I was making last-minute preparations to meet a friend of a friend who lived there.

Dad had grown up with the Carruth family. J. C. Carruth and his wife, Emily, still live in Santa Rosa County. J. C.'s brother George made a career in the Navy, however, and with his wife Clara, lived in exotic places all over the world. I met George and Clara in San Diego, the home port for my small ship, the frigate O'Callahan. Giving me the name of his friend, Mr. Chao, in Kaohsiung, he asked me to send his greetings should my ship call on that port.

Mr. Chao, he explained, would be near retirement age. He was the custodian for the "China Fleet Club," a safe haven for U.S. sailors in that port. As most of the crew gazed in landstruck awe at the sights, smells, and sounds of the "sailor district," I made inquiries to find Mr. Chao. Once I had made myself clearly understood to some Chinese ears, Mr. Chao made his appearance with a broad grin. I passed greetings to him from Mr. Carruth.

The meeting led to dinner at his home in a part of Kaohsiung where caucasians are never seen. I was as much the attraction as were the puppets and firecrackers at a "Punch and Judy" show. I attended a "Ninja-style" movie with his son, Chia, where the audience competed with the screen for noise and attention. Chia gave me a tour of the area that few could imagine. I rode about Southern Taiwan on the back of a motorcycle, amazed at everything in view. I dined with Mr. Chao's nephew, a physician. Bonds were formed across a wide ocean of culture. It was a time I will never forget and for which I will always be grateful.

In my time at sea, with the crew of the O'Callahan, I never felt too far from family. We visited Kaohsiung several times, and each time was a homecoming. Mr. Chao and his family made sure of that. They were quick to note when "Number 1051" was in port.

My annual Christmas card from Taiwan is a treasure. It reminds me that there is a large family of people the world over who are our friends—if only we are privileged to meet them. I hope everyone in the service has access to connections as good as those I had while I served. It made the trip a great deal more bearable.

Admittedly, coming from a small town like Chumuckla, where everybody knows everybody or knows somebody who knows everybody or knows somebody who knows somebody who knows everybody, is a distinct advantage.

$$\oint\oint\oint\oint\oint\oint$$

SILENT NIGHT AT MY SISTER'S HOUSE

My sister, Wanda Roberts, is married to a Navy flyer. They live in Pensacola, Florida, the cradle of Naval Aviation. She and John have four lively children. Six-year-old Wesley, their oldest, has more energy than Three Mile Island. His sister, and often nemesis, is Mary Beth—a corporate baroness in a four-year-old body. Following close behind is Anna Ruth, a diplomat, age two (and gaining fast). Naomi, who has not yet reached a single digit in years of age, is already practiced at winning friends and influencing people.

Christmas will soon be celebrated in their household. It will carry many of the same sounds, smells, and feelings you might associate with your own celebration of the "Mass of Christ's Birth." At their house, it will carry quite a few more.

Wanda is a sociable person. If she has only seven biscuits and a couple of sardines, she will invite all of her family (cousins, uncles, and aunts included), the neighborhood, and half the Navy in Pensacola to stop by for Christmas dinner. She will find a way to feed them all.

The children will provide the entertainment. No doubt about it! Wesley and Mary Beth will sing carols accompanied by the sound of loud banging on pots and pans, using "antique" toys that were brand new with batteries included only hours before. Anna and Naomi will provide a tumbling acrobatics show, using the Christmas tree as a diving platform.

Soon the noise level will approach that of a flight of "Blue Angels" in their supercharged F-18 Hornets, screaming over the herds of cattle lowing in the star-lit fields below.

At this point, the shepherds will come in, dressed as the Navy Air Command Choir. Since John is the director of the choir, it is not unlikely that he could arrange their appearance. Besides the exhibition at Wanda's house, they sing at other national events throughout the year.

Pop, Uncle Lamar Campbell, and Uncle Olyn Matthews (the three "Wise Guys") will be there to provide local color. Uncle Joseph Howell will sit quietly in a soft overstuffed chair, as the noise grows even louder, and rest much as his namesake might have done a couple of thousand years ago.

Confusion and mayhem will reign as the joyous celebration continues.

As a finale, I expect the Naval Air Command Choir will sing "Silent Night." And with any luck, it *will* be at some point. The well-fed and content family of believers will seek out a warm niche to allow the multi-course meal to settle itself amid low discussions of warm tidings.

Wanda, Mom, Aunt Frances, Aunt Elizabeth, and Aunt Nina will start washing dishes.

We will not be there this year. I would have enjoyed visiting with all the relatives. And my wife would have been a great help cleaning up.

§§§§§§§

THE TAIL OF THE CHRISTMAS CALF

At one time Santa Rosa County was awash with small dairies. Thomas and Milton Salter had one just across the road from our place in Chumuckla. The Thomases had one on Allentown Highway. The Russell family ran a dairy in Fidelis. The Ted May Dairy was in Jay. Hubert Lowery's family dairy farm and the Smith family dairy farm were in Brownsdale. Carl and Ed Whitfield and Wilson Whitfield milked cows in Allentown. Sherman Taylor's farm was on Munson Highway. Roy Bray had a dairy for a number of years on County Highway 191—a mile or two east of the junction with County Road 197. There were more—the Paces, Penningtons, McDaniels, and

225

Lunsfords. Ezra Chavers had a rather large dairy south of Ward's Store. And in the Wallace Community, the McCaskills had a nice, small dairy.

They are all gone now.

Until recently, you could see a faded sign announcing McCaskill's Dairy on the end of the old dairy barn, facing Highway 147. The building is now in disrepair. The fences are gone. Mr. McCaskill died a number of years ago. Mrs. McCaskill retired from teaching first grade at Pace School. She still lives in the house next to the remains of the old barn.

J. D. McCaskill cared meticulously for his herd. He tried his best to control flies and keep the system in prime condition for his cows. Apparently, however, there was one time too many when a cow slapped Mr. McCaskill with her tail as she tried to discourage a determined fly. That incident led to a total herd of bob-tailed Holsteins and Jerseys.

The bob-tailed herd presented an odd sight to passersby. The rare fly who ventured into the herd was attacked mightily by an army of imaginary tails. Stubby vestiges of the original tails quivered in search of a target. Bereft of their natural instrument of defense, the cows required a human interest in scientific fly control. J. D. kept them at bay with dust and sprays. He appreciated the cow's problem, but he needed his own satisfaction (sans tails) as well.

Some who had never had their face attacked by a moist, matted, cow's tail on a cold December morning failed to appreciate the practicality of J. D.'s solution. Mrs. Enfinger, Mrs. Lee, and Mrs. Mason, who prepared our school lunches, aired suspicions that the McCaskill family had developed a taste for ox-tail stew. J. D. and Melba's daughters (Mariane, Jill, and Jane) have tried to suppress those rumors for years.

Just before Christmas 1960, I made a decision to enter the cattle business. I visited Mr. McCaskill in search of a young calf. If he did not need a calf for a replacement in the milking herd, I would perhaps find a bargain for a family milk cow. In addition, the heifer might become the "seed stock" for the "Vic Campbell Cattle Ranch."

Mr. McCaskill and I talked about it for a spell—boy to man. We spoke about weather. We talked about cattle. We discussed pasture, fertilizer, and crops. I made an offer of $20 for one of his calves. He chewed on my offer.

Mr. McCaskill concluded that the $20 would not leave him with satisfaction. In the spirit of the Christmas Season, he proposed to make me a gift of the calf.

I was thankful. And, I was pleased with my Jersey calf. I fed her powdered milk and raised her to maturity. She produced several offspring. Some were heifers. They added to my seed stock. Some were bulls, destined to be steers— they added to my bank account. I purchased my second dairy calf from the Thomas Dairy. My herd began to expand exponentially—as did the work load.

For a number of years, I milked my cows and put fresh milk in our refrigerator. I have experienced a wet cow's tail in the face on an icy cold December morning before school. I often thought of the pleasure it would give me to cut off that cow's tail. But, I never did.

When I joined the Future Farmers of America, I had a ready-made "Greenhand" project—my cows. When the time came to go to college, I hade a ready-made bank account—my herd. I sold my cattle business when I started college. The money I made from the sale paid for about a year of school. The "Vic Campbell Cattle Ranch" was never to be though. I studied all manner of subjects that would help me to avoid ever having to milk a cow again...(I hope).

I can imagine Mr. McCaskill would be pleased to know his Christmas gift became a part of my college tuition. It might also make him happy to know that someone else appreciated his solution to the problem of the cow's tail.

§§§§§§§

X

Another View

Contributed Writings by
Dianne Hatfield Cummings and Coleman G. Wade, Jr.

"Experience is a grindstone, and it is lucky that
we get brightened by it—not ground."

Josh Billings

"We cannot afford to forget any experience,
even the most painful."

Dag Hammarskjold

"What one has not experienced,
one will never understand in print."

Isadora Duncan

"The holy passion of friendship is of so sweet and steady and
loyal and enduring a nature that it will last through a whole
lifetime, if not asked to lend money."

Mark Twain

MORE COTTON PICKERS

A fortunate schedule of business travel allowed me to spend a recent Saturday with friends in Dallas. I met with Joyce Hatfield and her sister, Dianne Cummings. Joyce and Dianne are sisters who—with their many brothers, sisters, and cousins—experienced a quest for knowledge in the "government surplus green" halls of Chumuckla School. Their large family is still a respected part of that community.

Joyce and Dianne have found a measure of success in the business world. Dianne is a Commercial Loan Supervisor, overseeing a portfolio of more than a billion dollars. (I thought numbers like that were only used in conjunction with the government budget.) Joyce is a Senior Underwriter for retail mortgages throughout a several-state region of the Midwest.

They are both beautiful women, who dress with impeccable taste. They carry an air of executive authority. They are businesswomen that get the job done.

Dianne told me that she thinks the people she supervises actually believe she was born in a business suit and always had self-confidence. Few would believe she is an ex-cotton picker. She recalled that, when she was a child, her mother placed her on the cotton sack, pulling both she and the cotton behind her through the long, dusty rows. The ever-present gnats would pester her eyes as the sweat beaded up on her face and dampened her hair. She remembers the maddening slap of an occasional malevolent cotton plant.

When she and Joyce were a little older, they joined other children in the area to help a relative or friend to harvest their cotton. They remember wearing flour-sack dresses to the fields. They remember the refreshment of cold ice water. They remember the hard work of their parents, older brothers and sisters, uncles, aunts, and cousins. It is a warm remembrance.

I have talked with a few ex-cotton pickers lately. I am beginning to wonder whether picking cotton in one's youth is a requirement for achievement in adulthood.

Joyce, for all her business-like appearance, is a closet artist and photographer. Dianne, the astute businesswoman, is a closet writer. I confess to reading some of her "farm-girl" memoirs during my visit.

Joyce made a trip home awhile ago. She traveled about the county and photographed some of the "memories" we talked about. She also worked with her family and friends to collect some old photographs of people and places in the county that are special. Some of the photographs she made and borrowed from friends are a part of this book.

I convinced Dianne to share some of her work in this book. Farm girls often have a different perspective on life than do farm boys. Her contributions are contained in the next few sections.

$$\text{\textphi\textphi\textphi\textphi\textphi\textphi\textphi}$$

TOM THE ROOSTER AND ME
(by Dianne Hatfield Cummings)

I rolled over and put my pillow over my head, trying to drown out the shrill noises coming from my bedroom windowsill. "Tom, go away! It's Sunday morning, and I don't want to wake up yet!" I cried from under my pillow. The shrill but proud yell attacked the still morning air once more. I knew all my pleading was in vain. Tom was ready for his early morning corn, or figs, or whatever else he might demand of me. But whatever the treat, it had to be hand-fed. After all, Tom had done his job, as all good roosters do at the first ray of sunlight. He alerted the whole neighborhood that it was time to begin a new day. Now he was a hungry bird. He wanted his just rewards.

I poured out of bed and pulled on my cotton "flour-sack" dress. I tied the big sash in the back. Without shoes or combed hair, and no thought of being a prim and proper little girl, as all six-year olds should be, I slipped quietly down the hall. I secretly passed through the back screened door, trying not to wake my sleeping brothers and sisters. I ran barefoot across the dew-damp grass and headed for the corn crib. Tom met me there and stationed himself right behind my heels. He knew the treat that was to come.

I climbed into the crib and grabbed a fat ear of yellow corn. Then I ran for the fig tree. What happened next must have been a strange sight. I scrambled up that tree with all the agility of a wild animal in the jungle. Tom flew to his perch on the highest possible limb he could reach. However strange this scene must have appeared, it was a weekend ritual for Tom and me—and would be the same each weekend day that summer.

Weekdays were an exception. I went into the fields at the crack of dawn with my mother to pick vegetables for the family freezer. On those days Tom followed the long vegetable rows with me. I shelled peas and other garden delights for him.

Once we were seated on our fig tree perches, I picked individual kernels of corn from their corncob home and fed them to Tom one at a time. I plucked the ripe, juicy fruits of the fig tree for myself and ate them.

Tom did not want to be given his breakfast in a normal manner. We played games with those golden little morsels. I would place a kernel on my nose; Tom would peck it off. I put them on my tongue as though I were going to eat them myself. He pecked at my cheeks until I opened my lips. He took his breakfast directly from my mouth. My favorite trick was to place little kernels between my toes. I let Tom peck them away. It tickled, causing me to giggle.

« »

"Dianne, don't you fill up on those figs now!" Mother yelled out the kitchen window. "These hot biscuits will be ready in a minute. Now you come on down out of that tree before I cut me a switch!" When Momma threatened with "the big stick," the whole family knew it was time to get serious. However, she threatened me like this every Saturday and Sunday morning that entire summer. She never followed through.

Sometimes I thought Momma just scolded because it was expected of a mother. It was as if she knew that out of her nine little Indians, at least one of us had to be doing something we shouldn't do. I remember Momma yelling, "You young'uns are too quiet. What are you into?"

"Nothin' Momma," was our usual reply, as we ran out the back door with our hands full of tea cakes. Invariably, it was just before supper.

I climbed down off my tree when the smell of freshly baked biscuits filled my nostrils. Tom followed and sat on the back porch rail while I ran into the kitchen. I could easily devour two huge syrup and butter biscuits by myself, but Tom knew that I would save a small portion of my feast for him.

232

"Now you young'uns eat your breakfast and get out of my kitchen so I can start my Sunday dinner. You know your aunt and uncle will be here any minute," my mother demanded. On Sundays, Aunt Jesse and Uncle John were like comfortable pieces of furniture in our house. They had been coming for Momma's special fried chicken and chocolate cake for as long as I could remember.

I liked to see them come. My tall, skinny aunt would sit on the back porch with her mouth full of snuff and watch Tom and me put on a show. We had especially good fun after Sunday dinner. That is when Aunt Jesse sat her full, contented body down in the rocking chair on the back porch. She took off her shoes and stretched out her long legs for a doze in the sunshine. I was enthralled with Auntie's feet. She had very crooked toes. In some places, she had no toes at all. Aunt Jesse was forever telling me how she cut them off while playing with an axe. "Little girls should never play with axes," she admonished in a believable voice.

I sat and watched Aunt Jesse doze until she finally converted to a full snore. I did not want her to sleep. I was impatient for her to wake up so the "Tom and Dianne Show" could begin. In desperation one day, I ran to the corncrib and grabbed an ear of corn. Tom, of course, followed close behind with hungry expectation. I removed some kernels from the ear. I quietly slipped onto the back porch and squatted beside Auntie's feet.

For what I was about to do, I knew "the big stick" was a clear possibility. But I just could not resist the wicked temptation. I held Tom back while I carefully placed the kernels of corn between her toes. Aunt Jesse never stirred. I ran with Tom and hid behind the porch. Then, when I was sure she had not awakened, I sat Tom on the porch. He ran for his "beak-watering" feast. Hidden behind the porch, but watching every move, I watched my Aunt go into a complete and uninhibited frenzy. She started kicking her feet. She screamed, "Hallelujah, bless my soul, he's gonna eat the rest of my toes. Oh Lord! Somebody get this chicken off of me before I have some chicken and dumplin's for supper!"

It didn't take long for my father to come to his sister's rescue. I think that is what saved the "tannin of my behind." Had it been mother "busting" through that door, my tender hide would have been doomed. My father, on the other hand, let out a howl of laughter. The sight of the commotion around the rocking chair was homemade comedy. Auntie jumped around like she was standing on hot coals. Every time a foot touched the ground, Tom would take a peck. Picture it yourself. Aunt Jesse's crooked toes just kind of wrapped themselves around the corn kernels and wouldn't let go.

But Tom was determined to get his corn!

I stayed hidden most of the afternoon. I waited until things were back to normal. I was very proud of what I had done because of the laughter it gave my father. I knew, even then, it was an event he would bring up at family reunions to come. And the story would get better with every telling.

« »

Later in the afternoon, another aunt and uncle dropped by. They were from the city. Along with them was my cousin, a girl. She was about my age. I loved my cousin dearly, even though she had all the things I could only dream of. She had shining golden hair. She always wore lacy dresses. And she always, always wore her shoes and socks! I supposed this was because she was a city girl.

I, on the other hand—I was a farm girl inside and out. I only brushed my hair when Momma strapped me under the back porch water faucet. With soap in hand, she tried in vain to make me look like cousin Mandy in a single thirty-minute sitting. The ordeal was useless, of course. I still would not put on my shoes or scrub the dirt off my elbows and knees. And I had never owned a lacy dress in my short life.

Mandy loved to come visit. We played until the sun went down. Sitting in the middle of the grass—on a blanket of course—I would listen to her many adventures while I fed corn to Tom. When I placed a little kernel of corn in my mouth for Tom to take from my tongue, Mandy was appalled. "Do you eat that nasty corn, the same corn you feed that chicken?" she asked disgustedly.

I started to open my mouth and let Tom take his treat, but another thought entered my head. "Of course I eat this corn. It's delicious!"—and I swallowed the kernel. "You mean you ain't never ate no raw corn? It's great!"—and I had another kernel.

I could see her curiosity building. I knew she had a strong temptation to place a kernel in her mouth. I knew as well that I had "lucked out" with the "Aunt Jesse Incident." My luck was running out, but I just could not resist the powerful temptation. "Go ahead," I urged, "you'll love it. Just put it on your tongue and taste how good it is."

In all the months of letting Tom take corn from my mouth, he had never hurt me or even scratched me. I had learned, however, to eventually open my mouth and let him have the corn. Mandy, on the other hand, did not understand the rules.

Just as she placed the kernel inside her mouth, Tom flew up and gave her a big peck on her lower lip. I never quite understood why he was not a little more patient with her, like he was with me. Somehow, I think it wasn't really the corn he was after. Maybe he was jealous of Cousin Mandy's company. Maybe he wanted all of my attention for himself.

If this was his plan, it worked.

After Mandy's earth-shattering scream, she removed her hand from her face. There, looking to me like Mt. Everest, was a welt on her lip. It totally distorted her beautiful face.

It took exactly twenty-seven seconds for her to run into the house and tell the whole nasty story in grisly detail to both her mother and mine. I stood on the back porch by the screen door holding Tom. I watched my hysterical cousin in action. I could have run and hid. I wanted to. But I knew it would be useless. My mother knew all of my hiding places. And, if I did run, my punishment would be even worse.

After it was all over I thought, "Now that wasn't so bad." I had "lucked out" again, because Momma, following a ritual, had let me cut my own switch. I brought back the smallest one I could find that could still be considered a "switch."

"This one ain't big enough; you go get me a bigger one," she said. "But Momma," I pleaded, "all the big ones are high in the tree, and I can't reach them."

We both knew I could climb that tree like a starving monkey after a ripe coconut. For some reason known only to Momma, she accepted my response. The punishment commenced using the small switch. I did a lot of extra howling and jumping around. In a thoughtful way, I wanted her to be satisfied that the small switch had done the job.

With nightfall my busy day ended. I crawled into bed early. Tom was sitting on my windowsill as the sun rested behind the pine trees. I lay there thinking of how the summer was going to last forever.

I knew when summer was over I had to begin school. I was immensely unhappy about it. It meant each and every day I would have to put on shoes and brush my stringy dark brown hair. The thought depressed me. Summer days flew wonderfully by with just Tom and me and our daily rituals.

« »

It was nearing summer's end when, one Saturday afternoon, Aunt Jesse and Uncle John stopped in. This was unusual, I thought. They were a day early.

My mother called me to come inside. I was to help her get my clothes ready for school. School would begin the following week. I did not want to be inside on my last Saturday of summer. Momma gave me no choice. I stood impatiently while she fitted dresses and shoes. She decided which dresses I could wear and which ones she would use for quilt scraps.

Momma took altogether too much time. I was dying of curiosity. What were Daddy and my uncle doing outside, in the barnyard? I wanted to join them. Momma refused to let me go. She firmly ordered me to stay inside for the rest of the afternoon and help her in the house. I did as I was told until my young temperament could stand it no longer.

Momma grew intense as she sewed a patch on one of my dresses. The moment allowed me to wander quietly onto the back porch. I slipped out the door and into the barnyard without being noticed.

I stood frozen in horror as I saw what my father and my uncle were doing. Daddy held a chicken by the neck, twisting it over and over. I had seen this done before; it was always done in preparation for Sunday dinner. This time was different, however. Lying there on the ground in a lifeless form was Tom.

The horrifying scene seared my thoughts and brought within my soul a fit of rage. I flew into my father with all the passion and energy that forty-five pounds could express. I hit him and I screamed. He grabbed me by the shoulders and held me.

"Sister, listen (Daddy called all his daughters sister), these chickens are sick. There is a disease spreading in this area, and all the chickens are dying. Tom was sick. He was hurting. I had to put him out of his misery." He was pleading for my understanding.

Momma came running through the barnyard gate. She was shocked. Her job was to keep me inside until the unpleasant duty was completed. She had not noticed that I was outside the house until she heard my screams.

I looked at her. I looked at my father. Then I looked at Tom, lying on the ground. At that moment, I ran as hard and as fast as I can ever remember. I do not remember making the distance across the three open fields. I do not remember crossing several fences. I do remember at last that I was in the neighbor's corn patch. My mother and father begged me to stop, but I didn't. They could not keep up with me.

I ran deep into the corn patch where I knew I could not be found. I crawled under some thick vines that almost created a cave. I lay there in the dirt. I cried so hard I grew sick. I saw visions of Tom sitting on the Sunday dinner table.

My parents had a difficult chore to provide food for all their children. Aunt Jesse and Uncle John were even worse off. Knowing this was of little consolation, with my dear pet, Tom, lying cold and dead in the barnyard.

I wasn't sure I believed the story about the disease. It really didn't matter. Tom was dead. Eventually, I cried myself to sleep, remaining in my little cave for the rest of the afternoon.

Voices from a short distance behind woke me. I could hear the voices of men and women calling my name. I could tell I had been asleep for a long time. The sun was setting. My vine-covered cave had darkened. My parents had rounded up the neighbors for an all-out search. I lay there for a long time, hardly breathing. I just listened to their pleas.

Finally, I heard Momma's voice. It was not one of pleading. It was a voice of desperation. I felt for her. She was hurting as much as I had hurt. I crawled out of my cave and walked in the direction of her voice. The look of relief on her face is one I will never forget. She picked me up. She brushed the dirt off my face.

Everyone gathered to take a long walk back home. There was much chatter going on around me, but I was completely silent in my mother's arms. We arrived in the barnyard. All of the people gathered around the chicken pen. "We have a surprise for you," my mother said. She opened the gate and I saw six white chickens sitting on the roost.

"Our neighbor, Mr. Reynolds, gave you all these chickens." I just looked down at the ground. I turned my back without a word and walked into the house. I don't know what happened to those six white chickens. I never went back to look at them.

Then school began. I awoke every morning, put on my shoes, brushed my stringy dark hair, and looked out the window. I stared at my bare windowsill. Several mornings I cried. But no one saw my tears. In time the hurt grew more bearable.

And school wasn't so bad. I began to look forward to putting on my shoes in the morning. I enjoyed brushing my hair until it shined. I even received a new hand-me-down from Mandy that just happened to be a lacy dress. I saved it to wear on special occasions.

I am a grown woman now and proud to be a lady. I will never forget those days of growing up in the country, though.

Most of all, I will never forget those especially memorable summer days with Tom.

And years passed before I ate fried chicken again.

§§§§§§

CHARLIE'S DEAD (by Dianne Hatfield Cummings)

"Charlie's dead." I'll never forget my Grandmother's words. Tears of pain ran down her face. Charlie was my first cousin— Grandma's first and only Vietnam victim.

Do you remember what you were doing when you heard the news of John Kennedy's death? That's a question you have all probably heard before. In fact, you surely remember the details of that moment. That's the way it was when I heard the news of Charlie.

It was late in the afternoon on a summer day. We had finished supper and were enjoying the last minutes of daylight outdoors. It was the typical hot, muggy, summer evening that Florida was famous for. There was hardly a breeze blowing, and the crickets were becoming increasingly noisy as the sun settled behind the tall pine trees.

I was following behind Mother and Daddy as the walked up and down the long vegetable rows in our family garden. Occasionally, they would stop and pull a week or pluck an overripe tomato before it rotted on the bush. Our family garden always looked hand-manicured and very fruitful. This was important to my parents, as it was usually our only source of food.

"Hey, there's Sarah and Dave," said Mother in a tone that clearly reflected surprise. "I wonder what they're doing here in the middle of the week." Aunt Sarah and Uncle Dave lived in the next town and often came to visit on Sunday afternoons, but very seldom on the weekdays.

I looked up as they drove into the yard. "Granny is with them," I said. I could hardly see the top of her head as she sat huddled in the back seat of the automobile—like a child with her hair tied in a little bun on top of her head.

"Hey! Ya'll get out and come on in!" yelled Daddy as they pulled into the yard and began opening car doors. "Come on out and I'll give you a job," Daddy said teasingly as though he would make them pick vegetables. Aunt Sarah and Uncle Dave were coming through the garden gate to join Mother and Daddy in the garden. I climbed over the fence and ran to meet Grandma as she was a little slower and dragging behind my aunt and uncle. I put my arms around Granny and gave her a big hug. I noticed she held on a long while and, when she let me go, I looked down and saw tears in her eyes. "Charlie's dead," were her only words. Nothing more needed to be said. No details were needed; no questions were necessary. Vietnam—that explained it all.

It had only been about two weeks before that Charlie had come bursting through our kitchen door on Sunday morning. "Aunt Evelyn, fix me a plate full of those biscuits and syrup; I came all the way from the jungle for this!" he said kiddingly. Then, as my mother was about to bring out a pan of hot, freshly baked biscuits, he walked over to the stove and gave her a big hug. Mother gave Charlie a big hug in return and told him to grab a plate. "You're getting much too thin," was my mother's reply as she put an arm around Charlie. It's true, Charlie had lost weight since his tour in Vietnam. He still maintained the appearance of the Charlie I grew up with though—a plump, light-haired rosy-cheeked farm boy whose goal in life was to pick on people and chase girls. We all loved him dearly because he was a down-to-earth, unpretentious cut-up. Charlie was always laughing and always, always hungry.

This was Charlie's first leave home from the war. Out of all the hundreds of "Hatfield" clan, he was the only member that had gone to Vietnam. There were a lot of females in the family who did not qualify for the draft. Charlie did have a brother-in-law, Carlos, who was drafted into the army and served part of his time at the same time as Charlie.

Little did we know, that Sunday morning, that this would be the last time we were ever to see or visit with Charlie. Even though his tour was almost completed, he was to return to Vietnam the following day for his last few months of duty.

I heard my mother's cry from the garden behind me. I knew Aunt Sarah and Uncle Dave had just broken the news. I should have gone to my mother's side to comfort her, but I didn't. I walked away from Granny and headed for the barn loft to hide my tears. Memories began to run through my mind as I recalled my earlier days of growing up with Charlie always around. I remembered that many times he would come by our house late on summer afternoons in his truck and ask my mother if he could take me and my brothers and sisters to "the old gully" for a swim. I think he hated to see us having to work day in and day out in the field, trying to cope with the hot, sticky climate. We would run excitedly to grab the necessities for a swim in the creek the moment our mother gave her approval.

The old Gully (a.k.a. Sand Ditch) was the swimming hole for most of the children in the county. There was an old tree leaning out over the cold, clear-running water. A rope with several knots in it was tied from the biggest branch on this tree. The big joy at Sand Ditch was to climb onto the bank on the other side of the lake by way of the enormous tree roots, which were partially exposed in the water. Once you were on the upper bank you would grab the knotted rope, climb as high was you had the "guts" for, and swing out over the water, ending in a big dive off the rope into water so cold it would take your breath away. Charlie was the "rope champion." He could climb higher and swing out farther than anyone in the county. He was my hero.

There was one occasion at the old gully when I thought, at the age of thirteen, that I could do as well as the boys who were showing off with their rope tricks. I began swimming across the deep water to climb the roots onto the bank. At first, I wasn't sure what had happened when I felt the cramp in my leg. I tried to swim farther, but my leg wouldn't cooperate. I began to panic. There was so much screaming and laughter, I thought no one could hear my cries for help. I remember going under for the third time before I was being pushed up from the dead, cold water into the bright, sunny air.

"You're supposed to swim *on top* of the water," Charlie kidded, as he held a secure arm around my waist and headed for the dry bank. He helped me up the tree roots and onto the river bank. He sat down beside me and put an arm around my shoulders. "You okay?" he asked, concerned.

"I think so," I replied, as I gasped to catch my breath. I wasn't sure why Charlie didn't carry me back to the shore as opposed to taking me across to the deep side. This meant I would have to swim back, and I was afraid to get back into the water. "I don't want to swim back," I said. "I'm afraid I'll get another cramp in my leg."

"You don't have to worry about that," Charlie said. "When you jump off the rope you'll be half way across."

"I don't want to jump off the rope. I'm afraid."

"Nonsense," said Charlie. "You've heard the old saying that if you fall off a bicycle you should get right back on." He hoisted me up and pulled me toward the edge so we could grab the rope when it swung back. "Now, lets show all these fellows that you are better than them," he urged.

I was afraid, but I felt more confident with Charlie there. We climbed the rope together. People were laughing and urging us on. Charlie pushed me farther up the rope so that I could stand on his shoulders. This forced me almost to the top of the rope. We swung out a couple of times, and I dove into the water from Charlie's shoulders with him jumping right behind me. He followed me to the shore to make sure I was safe. When I came out of the water everyone was cheering. I felt great. Charlie had given me back my confidence —and then some.

I also remembered the times I would spend the night with my cousin Faye, Charlie's younger sister. We would want to sleep in Charlie's bed as youngsters because he would tell the greatest ghost stories.

The white convertible was another instance that came to mind. Charlie, as a high school senior, had bought his first automobile. I don't remember the make or model, but it was white, with a convertible top. He loved it. Charlie always took the time, however, to pick me up on Sunday afternoons and take his little sister and me for a ride. He always seemed to enjoy showing off for us.

And then there were all the camping trips. My oldest brother, Bobby, and Charlie would oftentimes take Faye and me along with them on their camping trips. They never seemed to mind having their "little sisters" along. It could have been, however, that we would do the cooking for them and clean the dishes later. These were the times when Faye and I thought our big brothers would always be there.

That wasn't the case. Charlie's life ended abruptly from a single bullet in the chest, and Bobby died many years later, as he just seemed to grow tired of living. Both are missed more dearly than they could ever have imagined.

I watched from my upstairs bedroom window as the helicopter settled on the baseball field. It had taken several days for Charlie's body to reach home, accompanied by Carlos, his brother-in-law, also a Vietnam soldier. Before the body ever reached our little town to rest forever, the Army had sent someone out to speak to the family on all the details of Charlie's death and to convey their regrets. The only place the helicopter could land in our little town was on the high school baseball diamond. It happened that our two-story farmhouse was across the street from the field, and from my bedroom window, I watched the sad details of the next hour—an event I am sure was taking place in grief-stricken homes all across America.

I could see my uncle standing in the dugout, waiting for the helicopter to land. It was raining. I could hardly make out my Uncle Roy's outline through the steady downpour. He looked thin and beaten. I'm not sure to this day where my Aunt Velvie, Charlie's mother, was at the time. Maybe she was waiting in the schoolhouse across the street. The main picture that will stick in my mind forever, though, is Uncle Roy standing in that dugout with the rain pouring down around him. Occasionally, I could see a puff of smoke as he inhaled his cigarette.

The man in uniform ran from the helicopter into the dugout to avoid the rain. I watched as he and my uncle shook hands and stood there conversing for awhile. I didn't watch any longer. I'm sure they left to join Aunt Velvie and tell her what a "good soldier" her son was and that he died bravely.

The funeral was a few days later. I can't ever recall so many people crowded in a church or at a grave site. The entire community must have come to pay their respects to its first Vietnam casualty.

A war, a small town, a funeral—the scenario for many Americans during the Vietnam era. And I am sure that, as with Charlie, someone still grieves the death of all those young soldiers and remembers those first words—just as I did when I heard "Charlie's dead."

§§§§§§§

THE STORE (by Dianne Hatfield Cummings)

Growing up in a small town allows moments of pleasant memories. One in particular often refreshes my mind. I see the little, white, wood-framed, two-room building in beautiful "downtown" Chumuckla. It is a place known to all who stop in, now and then, as "The Store."

With its unfinished wooden floors and slamming screen door, "The Store" is little competition for any of the major convenience stores. However, there is not a convenience store in existence that can compare with the down-home atmosphere of that little two-room haven of delights.

Enter "The Store." There is a counter immediately to the left. On top of the counter are an adding machine and a cash register. They fit comfortably there with the aging decor of their surroundings.

A freezer next to the counter displays a rainbow of frozen treats. Over the years, the glass front of this freezer has been adorned with small dirty hands and tiny noses beaded with

246

perspiration (including my own). Noses are pressed against the surface of the glass as tummies with minds of their own try to decide which color of the rainbow will give the greatest satisfaction.

In the back there is another freezer. In it are giant slabs of bacon, luncheon meats, and cheeses. They can be sliced on the spot and wrapped in white, waxy, freezer paper.

In the far right corner stands a timeless red ice box. On the front, emblazoned for all to see are the words "Coca-Cola." It contains icy-cold drinks for all those who wish to partake of carbonated refreshments.

The middle aisles are wooden shelves that contain potted meat, sardines, saltine crackers, and (bless us all) Moon Pies. This is the standard menu for the Saturday fishermen who stop by to stock up before heading for the Chumuckla swamps. Even a cricket cage stands in the back of the store. You can buy fish bait at the same time you are loading up on sardines and crackers. Out front, you can gas up your boat.

I invested my summers running barefoot to the store, a nickel in my hot, sweaty, little hand. I wanted to spend my fortune on one of those strawberry ice cream cones that was piled so high it would almost topple over. Half the time, I would be in such a hurry I would stub my toe on the pavement. Half a toenail would disappear. Little drops of "toe blood" marked my trail as I hobbled the rest of the way toward my vision of heaven.

This past summer I revisited the "The Store." My younger brother took me for a day of fishing, "Chumuckla Style." It has been twenty years since I left home, but the store has hardly changed. Trucks that pulled fishing rigs were lined up outside in the parking area. Farmers sat about on the wooden benches in front of the store. They talked about the weather, and the weather, and the weather.

The ice cream freezer, the "coke" box, and the cricket cages were all in their original locations.

It is comforting to know that after years of city hassles I can still go back there and once again be the little girl of years ago. When nobody was looking, I pressed my nose against the glass and marveled at the ice cream.

Which color of the rainbow would I choose today?

⸕⸕⸕⸕⸕⸕⸕

"JUNIOR" WADE LIVES

This letter was recently sent to me by my boyhood friend/ rival. I thought it a good addition to my "guest" writer section:

Dear Vic:

Please find enclosed one Duncan Gold Award transparent gold yo-yo. Take it out of the package and try it out. Examine it carefully and let your memory drift back to February 1962. We were in the seventh grade. Mr. Stafford was our teacher.

Lots of kids had yo-yo's (you know, the painted wooden kind that only went up and down, up and down). But you and I had Duncan yo-yo's. They cost a whole dollar. You could do tricks with them if you read the package directions carefully and watched the yo-yo man's demonstrations on the Lynn Tony TV show that came out of Pensacola on Saturday afternoons. I'm sure you remember the yo-yo man. He alternated Saturdays with the one-legged golfer.

Yo-yo's became a craze at Chumuckla school. Everyone imitated the yo-yo man before, after, and often during class. Mr. Stafford had to put a stop to this "toying" around. He announced there would be a contest the following Tuesday to determine the yo-yo champion, and then we would have to put our yo-yo's away for the rest of the year.

I know I could win that contest easily. I had a terrific blue Duncan Imperial and I never missed the yo-yo man.

On Friday, February 2, I had to stay home from school with a "relapse of the flu." On Saturday, February 3, my older sister broke my yo-yo string. (She never watched the yo-yo man.) It seemed fate was trying to rob me of my destiny as yo-yo champion. On Monday, February 5, I returned to school. You very generously gave me some yo-yo string and I was back in the game.

I could hardly sleep that night. In my mind, I practiced every yo-yo trick I knew over and over and over. Morning finally came, and for once I couldn't wait to get to school. After the bell rang and the roll was called, Mr. Stafford began the competition. We quickly eliminated all the other boy s in the class. It was down to you and me. As we stood in front of the class, I glanced over at your transparent gold yo-yo. It was pretty neat. You could see the string wound inside. But I had complete confidence in my blue imperial.

Mr. Stafford called for the first trick—a sleeper. My yo-yo paused at the bottom of the string for a good fifteen seconds. No problem.

The second trick was called for—rock the cradle. Again, no problem. I wound the string around my fingers and formed a cradle complete with rocking baby. The third trick was called walking the dog. Flawless again. It was as smooth as my mother's chocolate pie. Of course, you were performing all the tricks too.

Then the "biggie" was called for—around the world. I knew this one had to be executed with meticulous precision. I had to develop enough speed and rotation to make a giant loop and then recover my yo-yo. I looked over at you. You didn't smile. You wiped your sweaty palms on your pants leg and waited.

I spun my yo-yo out and up and off it flew into the air, barely missing someone's head. The string had broken. The class was in an uproar. Some thought it was funny. Some were sad for me and gave a collective "Ahhh-h-h." I looked back at you. What a smirk.

You had won the contest by technical default or by sabotage. You are the only one who knows for sure. Of course, you had won the right to say you had beaten me. I never held it against you though. In fact, after that contest, I bought another fifteen feet of string from you.

Many years ago, during one of our many moves, Brenda found a small diary in a trunk of keepsakes. She asked me what kinds of things would a young boy write in his diary. Being female, she thought it would hold secrets of first loves. We thumbed through the little green book together. Mostly, it documented the number of rats I had shot in the loft of the barn and the care and development of my beagle puppies.

The entry for Tuesday, February 6, 1962, stated simply, "Mr. Stafford let me yo-yo in front of the class." Merry Christmas, Vic. Happy yo-yo-ing, too...Junior

P.S. I got a red one this time!

ʄʄʄʄʄʄʄ

XI

Epilogue

"What peaceful hours I once enjoy'd! How sweet their mem'ry still! But they have left an aching void, the world can never fill."

William Cowper

WHERE DID THEY ALL GO?

The Chumuckla High School Class of 1967 is a microcosm of America. Our 20th reunion was a clarification of the fact. Some twenty members of the class, with their spouses and children, make a pretty fair picture of the Americans of 1987.

We had nine members serve in the military; five served in Vietnam. One member sells insurance today (successfully, too). One markets pharmaceuticals to physicians. Most have experienced unemployment. Some experienced business failure or the loss of a farm.

At least four of our class are in construction or married to people in the business. One is an electrician. One owns his own business, designing churches. We have a teacher, a crane operator, a marketing manager, and a plant foreman.

Most of the women became homemakers and mothers. One married a physician and runs the office. At least two sell real estate. One is a real estate analyst. Several keep books or otherwise manage their family businesses. One is a clerk.

Robert Winslow left the Navy as a well-trained diesel mechanic. He became a vice president of Mack Trucks. In 1986 Robert became our first casualty; he died suddenly of an aneurism in his brain.

Many of our group are active in their churches. Some are active in politics. It is no wonder; the history we waded through draws people to both of these areas.

All but one of our class is married now. Ellis Mayo, eligible bachelor, is holding out for the perfect woman. Sorry, Ellis, she's already taken!

Some former teachers attended the reunion. Mrs. Dobson (1st Grade) and Mrs. Stewart (4th Grade) were there and settled some long-standing disputes between students. (Paul did it!) After many years of teaching in Santa Rosa County, these two dedicated teachers have retired. Their schedules are almost filled now with reunion invitations.

Alice Guidy now heads up the Locklin Vo-Tech Center in Milton. She taught us how to type. For me, typing is a skill that paid off many times over. Alice and her husband, John, were career educators in the county.

Cal Bodenstein taught us (some) chemistry and coached a winning basketball team. Cal still teaches and runs a charter fishing boat on the side. Time was he could be found at Nichols' Seafood Restaurant on weekends, shucking delicious East Bay oysters. Oh, are those oysters fine!

Louise Driggers tried to teach English; in a few cases, she even succeeded! To this day, Louise is one of the most respected teachers of English in the county. You might find her coaching students in Shakespeare—"Friends, Romans, Countrymen: Lend me your ear. I come not to praise Caesar but to bury him. The evil that men do lives after them. The good is oft interred with their bones." Ol' Shakespeare had a way with words. Recently, she was promoted to Assistant Principal.

I wish some others could have joined us. Mrs. Bobbie Whitley (2nd Grade), John "Johnny Jet" Temple (Principal), Bill Massey (Guidance Counselor, now deceased), Margaret Campbell (Home Economics), "Plug" Walther (Vocational Agriculture), Bill Lundin (Physics), Leonard Stafford (Social Studies), "Preacher" Hunsucker, and others were *sorely* missed. I have personally been whipped by each of them!

§§§§§§§

Chumuckla School
Grades 1 - 12

Dovie Stewart
4th Grade Teacher

Ben Learns Fishing Tech-
nique From Grandpa

Methodist Church—Warmed
by the Rev. J. D. Renfroe

The school is now Grades K-6. Dovie Stewart retired in 1974. I never get to go fishing anymore, and the music in church will never be as good as when the Howell sisters sang, "I'll Fly Away—oh Lordy—I'll Fly Away."

Part of the 1957 Faculty   Part of the 1962 Faculty

Bus Drivers Rube Ard, Claude Jernigan, Troy White, and
Sidney Hayes—1957

The 1957 Faculty: Melba McCaskill, Bobbie Whitley, Ruth Childers, Dovie Stewart, James Lee, and Agee Brown. The 1962 Faculty: Mable Pitts, Gerald Martello, Ruby Massey, W. H. Massey, Margaret Campbell, and Norman Walther.

Hibiscus Esculentus Ready
for Market

Manning's Store in Milton—a
Customer

The Work Ethic Displayed by
This Crew (1957) Is All But
Gone—David Carswell, Carol
(Carswell) Bhide, and the
Author

Someone's Dream in the
1930s. This Barn Is Now
Abandoned

Santa Rosa County has an ideal all-year climate. While we do have some cold weather, we do not have blizzards and excessive cold.

It is possible to have winter gardens in which the hardier vegetables such as cabbage, turnips, lettuce, onions, collard, radishes, beets, etc., do well, as the ground seldom freezes sufficiently to kill the roots of such plants. The more tender vegetables are planted after February 15 through the summer, varying a little some years. The temperature seldom goes as low as 20 degrees and then for only a short time. The summer season is not oppressive, as we have abundant rainfall and nights are agreeable. We *never* have sunstroke, and outdoor occupations are not interfered with by the heat.

In 1930 the Board of County Commissioners summarized "Resources and Opportunities"

(contributed by Rusty Grundin)

Only Known Photograph
of Two-Toe Turnipseed
(seen here on the bulldozer
clearing new ground)

Pop had to have fresh vegetables or he would die!

The New Generation...Drinks in a can.
Jason and Christopher Gatewood With Wesley Roberts.

Temple's Store—north end of the county—
when men were men and women were proud
of it! Closed long before canned drinks.

W. R. Burgess and "Dew" Roberts—the
Burgess store. Mr. Roberts was the Sherrill
Oil distributor, later the "76" Oil Company

Cotton Gin Circa 1945. In the old days,
people had to work for a living.

258

Cuyler Herbert
Campbell

Bessie Swanson Savelle
Campbell

Jim Campbell

Dessie Howell Campbell

Cuyler married Bessie; brother Jim married Dessie. Cuyler
told the story. Floress Tinsley, a cousin to the Brown
twins, recalled it. The Joneses of Mulat are descended from
the Brown-Jones union.

Mae Brown Jones (ca. 1915)

Roy Jones (ca. 1943)

The Brown Twins—
Mae and Minnie
(ca. 1905)

Minnie Brown (ca. 1963)

The Robert Jones Family (1956)—
Robert, Frankie, Millie, Yvonne, Terry

In 1904 Jim and Cuyler (Grandpa and Great Uncle) Campbell found twin sisters to court (Minnie and Mae Brown). However, distance was a problem. Eventually my Grandpa found another lass (lots closer), and my Uncle made the trip alone. I am sure he was disappointed when the Brown girl turned her attention toward a young man named Jones. Several years later Cuyler's determined efforts at courtship won him the hand of Bessie Savelle. My cousins are the offspring of Cuyler and Bessie.

If Cuyler had married Mae, Roy had married Dessie, and Jim had married Minnie, none of us would be who we are now— and we might not even recognize us in the mirror!

Floress Burnett

The Howell Homestead

Sons of Cuyler and Bessie Campbell

The Howell Homestead was north of the Campbell Homestead and much closer than Mulat (on the Bay). Floress Maine Burnett was born in 1898, soon after the USS Maine blew up in Havana Harbor (died January '92).

The Cheerleaders Were Nice (1966)—R. to L.: Helen Hopkins,
Patsy Harris, Pam Patterson, Linda Ard, Janice Harris,
Brenda Davis, Lanell Robinett, and Sponsor Gladys Kirkland

9th Grade Officers
(1966):
Wayne Diamond,
Glenda Enfinger,
Dianne Hatfield
(3rd from left),
Brenda Hopkins,
Gail Cotton, and
Wayne Harris

Some of the 10th Grade (1962):
Rufus Ard, Ronald Castleberry, Donnie Davis,
Jerry Harris, Barbara June Hatfield, Charles Hatfield,
"Tubby" Jernigan, Ernestine Joiner, and Shirley Kelley.

Part of the 5th Grade (1957)

D. Andrews, R. Ard, J. Bell, A. Byrd, R. Castleberry, D. Davis, B. R. Enfinger, B. Enfinger, H. Freeman, G. Gavin, L. Harris, J. Harris, G. Holley, B. Hatfield, C. Hatfield, M. Hopkins, E. Jernigan, E. Joiner, S. Kelley, and W. Lee. Others: R. Lowery, E. Manning, I. McNac, J. Spears, C. Stewart, L. Stewart, V. Ward, J. Watson, P. White, T. Whitley

Part of the 1957 Football Team
(almost beat Jay once)

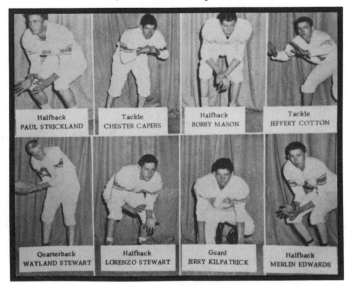

Halfback
PAUL STRICKLAND

Tackle
CHESTER CAPERS

Halfback
BOBBY MASON

Tackle
JEFFERY COTTON

Quarterback
WAYLAND STEWART

Halfback
LORENZO STEWART

Guard
JERRY KILPATRICK

Halfback
MERLIN EDWARDS

265

FFA Officers (1967): Wade Cox, Doug Horton, Wade Harris,
Jimmy Howell, Dale Holley, and Jackie Salter

Some Student Council Members Selling Pennants: Sandy Davis,
Judy Wyrosdick, Virginia White,Sharon Head, Diane Stevens,
Martha Walther, Molly Baggett...Randy Wolf, Jimmy Kimbrough

Bob Burgess (Ol' Robert)—in NBC-TV interview
in Jungles of Vietnam

Charlie (July 1966)—one of
14 victims of the Vietnam
War from our county.

Others

Howard Ard, Army, 1969
Richard Bray, Army, 1968
John Cannon, Army, 1968
Donald Gillman, Army, 1968
Billy Lamb, Army, 1966
Warren Lawson, Army, 1970
Robert Mason, USMC, 1967
William Mayhair, Army, 1966
Daniel Millen, Army, 1971
Edwin Schubert, Jr., Army, 1967
James Smith, Army, 1966
Clifford Wright, Army, 1969
Larry Yeuger, Army, 1970

Charlie's name is carved into the Vietnam Memorial in
Washington, D.C.

LIN C EUCKER · RONALD L FENSTERMACHER · HUGH C GALBRAITH · CHAR
W HARMON · WILLIAM H HAWKINS · ROBERT M HULSE · ROBERT M JOHN
R KITTLE · DENNIS C KNUTSON · NORMAN L KOOS · JOSEPH S KOPFLER Jr
ARLES G McINTOSH · RONDA LEE RAGLIN · JAMES K O'LEARY · RICHARD N
S R NASH · DAVID P SPEARS · PAUL J STRAUSSER · ROBERT L STUDARDS ·
MOND L TRUDEAU · CLIFTON B ANDREWS · WILLIS S BOWMAN Jr · DAN W
N BASS · DAVID CLEELAND · EVERETT A CURRENCE · ARTHUR H DYVIG Jr ·
ESUS FLORES · MICKEY RAY GRABLE · CHARLES D HATFIELD · SAMUEL L HU
LEO C LAWSON · ROBERT J LYSAGHT · ROBERT C MOORE · ROBERT R MYLE
E SCHUMACHER · BENNY SENA · MILES T TANIMOTO · PAUL P VANOVER ·
UM BRYANT Jr · JOHN E CHRISTIANSEN Jr · JOHN P HICKEY · MARVIN C KIL
NZO C MAULDEN · DALE W SCHMIDT Jr · STEVEN R SHERMAN · JOSEPH M
S WALKER · DANNY W WANAMAKER · JAMES W COLLINS · SHELTON L EAKI
EORGE E THREATS · JOSEPH F HUNT · JOE D KEGLEY · AGAPITO MOLINA Jr ·
RY L MOTT · JAMES L McCRYSTAL · MELVIN W McDOWELL · HAROLD W REIN
RRY L SCHEMEL · ECKWOOD H SOLOMON Jr · JACK J HIEBER · RUTHERFOR
D BACCUS · WILLIAM G MAIN Jr · ROBERT G MALONE · JOHN H McREE ·
POWER · MICHAEL R SAMSON · BENNY L SMITH · PHILLIP N TROUGHTON

Warren Renfroe's neph-
ew, Jimmie D. Ryals,
was killed in Vietnam in
1970. He is listed under
Michigan dead.

Airmen from the Navy
and Marine corps
trained in our county.

Many died in
training—not to mention
those who were the
casualties of combat.
They are all someone's
special memory.

Warren Renfroe at the
"City Cafe" (a WWII Vet)

268

Marines Land in Korea (ca. 1951)
Where Is Their Memorial?
[photo by John Brown, USMC (Ret.)—
combat photographer]

R. H. Kilpatrick (ca. 1968)
With Korea Years Behind, Pat Kilpatrick
Pursues His Rock-Hunting Hobby

Navy OCS—Newport,
Rhode Island—Class 7008
Golf Company

Stephanie Gainer Was
Commissioned in 1989

USS O'Callahan (DE-1051), A Fast Frigate, "Irish Song" Was
Decommissioned in 1989—The USSR Fell Apart Soon Afterward

The USS O'Callahan had two 5-inch guns. Destroyers were
used regularly in Vietnam for support of troops ashore.

Olongapo City, Phillipines (ca. 1972)

A Ticket to Disneyland
—a good deal for returning Vietnam Vets!

Tradition calls for a poem in every Navy logbook for the first watch of a new year.

The poem on the next page is rather crude, but the Junior Officer of the Deck from midnight to 0700 on that New Year's Day was not a poet.

(U.S. cease fire and final hostile action occurred 26 days later.)

Deck Log: USS O'Callahan (DE-1051)—1 Jan 1973 (000-0700)

The peace of a cease fire settles the night
While O'Callahan, in Task Group 75.9, cuts brown Tonkin water
  and makes it white;
At Northern Military Region One, Point Allison.

Our schedule is from COMSEVENTHFLT
For this third Navy quarter of '73
To make the system more complete,
He added here USS Morton, Rupertus, and Wiltsie
Plus Hollister, Tucker, and Blandy

CTG 75.9 rides the Morton (DD948);
  he is our SOPA and OTC.
He is the boss and controls our fate,
  in the fledgling hours of '73.

Yoke is set throughout the ship.
The condition of readiness is placed at III.
The enemy watches, so to give them the slip
Our vessel shows no navigational lights at sea.

The forward mount is ready to shoot, in support of friends—
  if they should ask
But the holiday spirit keeps most guns mute, and makes our job an easier
  task.

The gyro is quirked so we steer by magnet,
In station yellow until the gyro is able.
Power is from 1-Bravo boiler, for steam first rate,
And we steer using the starboard unit and cable.

She's a good ship and she fights well
To give us hope for a better age
When peace will reign and we can tell
Of O'Callahan and crew, who turned for history—another page.

JOOD Victor S. Campbell
Ens., USNR

Dinner at Grandma's (ca. 1966)
"Doc" Matthews, Grandma (Aunt Dessie to many),
Aunt "Sis" Matthews, and Aunt Lyda (Brett) Grant

The Old Cattle Chute at Grandpa's

1957 "Southern Gothic" Mom and Dad

At Grandma's House
on County Road 197
in 1955

The Author's Wife, Karen,
With Her Grandmother,
Lucille Williams Gatewood

Cousins and Siblings—Martha (Matthews) Trigg, Wanda,
The Author, Kittye (Campbell) Norris, Roger Matthews,
Faye (Campbell) Westfall, and Jim
(with Freida, The Wonder Dog)

Uncle "JB" by an Old Homestead
(near Noma, Florida)

Gordon and Steven Howell
Measure a "Giant" Pine Tree

Uncle "Duke"
Lamar Campbell

Uncle S. L. "Slim" Howell
of Bonifay, Florida (ca.
1956)

Ella Enfinger With Cousin
Alvin's Kids (ca. 1962)

"Sissy" Strickland—Ella's
Sister Was a Confectionery
Expert As Well (ca. 1988)

Neal Enfinger Grew Up!
Here With Wife Sandra,
Daughters Vanessa and
Christina. (Author's wife
Karen in back)—1990

Uncle Bobby Carswell's Marina Barbershop (ca. 1982)
[flanked by Otis Wynn (left) and A. T. Mixon (right)]

Conversation and Porches Become A Memory—Killed Off by
Air Conditioning and Television—Here, Some Old County
Homesteads Now Empty, With Porches Unused

The Penton Place
Jct. Highway 197 and Highway 90

This Porch Still Gets Some Use

Site of "The Great Noma Shootout"
Carswell Homestead in Noma, Florida

Aunt Marguerite and
Cecil Carswell

Uncle Joe and
Aunt Nena Howell

Cotton at the Old LeRoy Shell Homestead

Cotton picking machinery forced people out of *good* jobs
and into the corporate migrant manager pool.

Uncle "Tobe"
E. W. Carswell of
Chipley, Florida

"Skeeter" Howell of
Skeetersonian Museum
Fame—Come Visit

The Carswell Brothers (ca. 1947)
Uncles Cecil, R. V., Bobby, Tobe, and Malgram

Uncle Olyn (Doc) Matthews
With Mary Beth

Easter Harris,
Sling-Shot Davis, and
T. D. Salter—
Church Reunion (1982)

The Very Center of the Universe

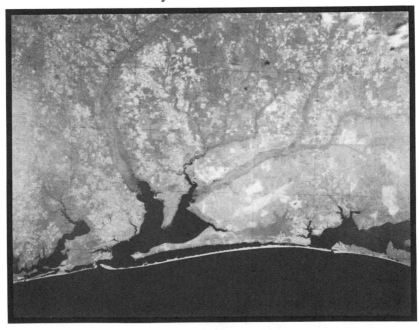

Copeland Griswold and Son Paul—
Selling Cotton in Jay

Campbell Salter Approaches The City Cafe

Salter's Farm Market on Hwy. 197

The Livestock Sale Barn

Lorenzo Howard—Corporate Executive With a
Major International Chemical Company

Co-Pilot For Commute
Dr. C. Yacomeni with son
Grant and Fish "Perchey"

Wilderness Lake in the
Kittatinny Mountain Range
(Not all of New Jersey is
urban.)

Australian Family Robson
Lee, "Mum," Lynette,
Lloyd (author's pen pal for 25 years), and Dennis

Cdr. John Roberts With Part of the
Navy Air Training Command Choir (Easter 1988)
Aboard the USS Lexington
(Brother-in-Law John is 2nd from left)

Jerry Kelley Had a Rude
Awakening! (Three Tours of
Duty in Vietnam)

"Junior" Wade
and
His Wife, Brenda
(True Americans)

Tim Burch

Cal Bodenstein

Alice Guidy

Louise Driggers

Paul and Joyce Stewart
(a new microwave oven)

Carol (Cook) Bryant,
Gary Lockett, and
Rhonda (Enfinger) Forte—
Reunion 1987

The Class of '67 in 1987
The Author, Paul, "Junior," Jerry, Ricky, Tim, Gary
Pamela, Faye, Paula, Nancy, Carol, Brenda, Rhonda, Karen

Mrs. Dobson
(First Grade)

Mrs. Stewart
(Fourth Grade)

Danny Holt, Danny Ellis, and Cynthia (Griswold) Nelson
Present a Gift to "Rusty" Grundin (Christmas 1965)

Uncle "Bo" Langham
Somewhere in France
(ca. 1918)

Uncle "Bo" Langham With
Granddaughter Katherine
(Howard) Frazier—Pensacola,
Florida (ca. 1953)

Ricky and Marian
(McCaskill) Hunsucker

Mutual Cousins of
Chumuckla
Ann (Jernigan) Tipton
(now a lawyer) and (at left)
Nancy (Howell) Wyatt

The Hatfield Home
For Many Years Was a Converted Barn

Jim Campbell
(author's brother—1956)

Mom With Daughter Wanda
(1957)

Wanda (Campbell) Roberts
(author's sister—1962)

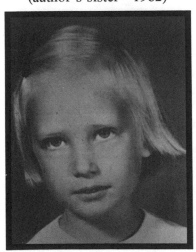

Curt and Letha Myers
Connoisseur's of Good
Oysters (1982)

Dianne (Hatfield)
Cummings—
Ex-Cotton Picker (1969)

Marina Dubrowin
"A Russian Spy"
(with the author)

The Artist, Nancy Akin
With Daughter Linzie
(January 1991)

Alexander Edward Campbell
With Admirers Allison and
Rachel Carter (1991)
The Saga Continues

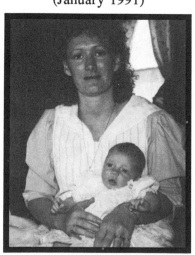